Overload
and
Boredom

Recent Titles in Contributions in Sociology
Series Editor: Don Martindale

OVERLOAD

AND

BOREDOM

*ESSAYS ON
THE QUALITY OF
LIFE IN THE
INFORMATION SOCIETY*

Orrin E. Klapp

CONTRIBUTIONS IN SOCIOLOGY, NUMBER 57

Greenwood Press
NEW YORK • WESTPORT, CONNECTICUT • LONDON

Library of Congress Cataloging-in-Publication Data

Klapp, Orrin Edgar, 1915–
  Overload and boredom.

  (Contributions in sociology, ISSN 0084–9278 ; no. 57)
  Bibliography: p.
  Includes index.
   1. Communication—Social aspects.   2. Communication—
Psychological aspects.   3. Entropy (Information theory)
4. Boredom.   I. Title.   II. Series.
  HM258.K554   1986   302.2   85–17532
  ISBN 0–313–25001–4 (lib. bdg. : alk. paper)

Library of Congress Catalog Card Number: 85–17532
ISBN: 0–313–25001–4
ISSN: 0084–9278

First published in 1986

Greenwood Press, Inc.
88 Post Road West
Westport, Connecticut 06881

Printed in the United States of America

The paper used in this book complies with the
Permanent Paper Standard issued by the National
Information Standards Organization (Z39.48–1984).

10 9 8 7 6 5 4 3 2 1

CONTENTS

Overload
and
Boredom

I

INTRODUCTION

This book is a collection of informal essays exploring the impact of information on the quality of life, especially the significance of boredom indicating dysfunctions of overloads of information, specifically in the directions of redundancy and noise. It aims to explain how a society could become boring in spite—indeed because—of huge loads of information. The information society is not only not immune but is susceptible to its own kinds of boredom, resulting from degradation of information in two ways, redundancy and noise, which outstrip the "slow horse" of meaning. It is a major paradox that growing leisure and affluence and mounting information and stimulation we call progress lead to boredom—a deficit in the quality of life. No small item of this deficit is attrition of meaning along with the vast accumulation of information. We also look into the function of social placebos supplying meaning that compensates for boredom and lack of meaning.

The essays extend some theoretical concepts in new ways, especially redundancy, resonance, noise, and entropy. I have tried to integrate these concepts in a systemic way, the main relations being that redundancy serves social resonance, but noise and dysfunctional redundancy interfere with resonance and both degrade information (that is, increase entropy) as loss of meaning. Together these concepts comprise a paradigm of information search.

The main theme is commonly called information overload, but our particular focus is on degradation, not merely increase in quantity, of information. Two main ways in which information degrades are explored.

The first is by becoming noiselike. We note that our information society is also a high-noise society. We live in a perpetual din of media, which we continually adapt to. Multi-media people listen with all their senses, trying to stay abreast of all developments. It is not at all unusual to have the television or radio on while reading a newspaper, eating breakfast, and now and then talking to somebody. We may also carry a watch or pocket pager whose beeping signals remind us to move along to new stimuli. We may also carry a cassette recorder ("ghetto blaster") as we walk down the street—adding to noise for everyone else—or wear a "Walkman," giving continual entertainment in our own sonic cocoon.

This is a high-input society. It seems that not a minute may be wasted in consuming commodities and communicating with as many people as possible. But in a Babel of signals, we must listen to a great deal of chatter to hear one bit of information we really want. We discover that information can become noiselike when it is irrelevant or interferes with desired signals, so tending to defeat meaning—making it harder to extract meaning from information, just as it is hard to extract metal from low-grade ore (in the language of Shannon and Weaver, 1949, too low a signal-to-noise ratio for messages to come through clearly). All too often, media and computers speed up the impact of information upon us without adding to its meaning for us. By taking in too much noise, a person becomes cluttered, not integrated. The result for our information society is that we suffer a lag in which the slow horse of meaning is unable to keep up with the fast horse of mere information.

The other main way in which information in large amounts degrades, according to our view, is by becoming sterile and redundant, helping to make life flat and insipid. I call this sort of degradation banalization.

Between those extremes of noise and banality, trying to stay on a meaningful course, society veers like a sailboat tacking in order to progress against the wind. Trying to understand this better, I introduce a paradigm of information search, showing that meaning and interest are found mostly in the *mid-range* between extremes of redundancy and variety—these extremes being called, respectively, banality and noise. Any gain in banality or noise, and consequent meaning loss and boredom, we view as a loss of potential, an increase of social entropy which subtracts from progress. Between banality and noise lie the desired goals, a balance of "good" (functional) redundancy with variety leading to discovery of more meaning.

In this view, boredom can come from either redundancy or variety when it does not tell enough of interest. The deficiency is not a sheer lack of information but hearing too much of what we are not interested in. That is, boredom as we experience it today is more likely to be from an *over*load than an underload.

Because boredom signals fading interest, it means a loss of human potential, for a certain line of action at least; and loss of potential is one definition of entropy (Boulding, 1978). By-products of boredom, such as low morale, thrill seeking, gambling, drug abuse, vandalism, and crime are loss of potential. So the ultimate focus of this book is not on boredom per se, which is merely a symptom, but degradation of information increasing entropy of modern society in spite—and to some extent on account—of its large information load.

Today we have an unprecedented flood of communication bringing us an information economy with many benefits yet to be realized. However, our enthusiasm for computers and the age of information should be tempered by warnings of the "limits to growth" literature about diminishing returns, diseconomies of scale, entropies of energy use, ecological damage, and environmental degradation. The upshot is that the more centralization and bigger the throughput of energy, the faster we go down the entropy chute.

If that is how it is on the *physical* side of the environment, why should it be different with the symbolic, with information? Dare we assume that more is always better in the case of information? Already problems of banality, noise, and information overload in modern society are recognized—omens of more to come.

This book holds that nothing exempts information from the Second Law of Thermodynamics, which asserts that matter and energy tend to degrade to more probable, less informative states. Just as energy degrades, so do information and culture. And the larger the amounts of information processed or diffused, the more likely it is that information will degrade in ways to be described here, on one hand toward meaningless variety, sometimes characterized as noise or information overload; and, on the other hand, toward sterile uniformity.

This concept of entropy—especially the idea that information itself degrades—is opposed to the idea of progress. They are opposed because, on the one hand, the idea of progress assumes that as knowledge advances, human well-being and happiness follow. On the other hand, the theory of entropy asserts that disorder and confusion tend to increase in spite of the best that humans can do—though vigilant effort can abate entropy for a time in a particular place. This opposition of entropy to progress is especially so if information itself is subject to entropy, for according to the idea of progress, the accumulation of information will sooner or later solve problems and benefit mankind. But what if this is not always so? If information itself is subject to entropy, then this doesn't follow at all. The progress idea has no place for the thought that advancing knowledge could increase human dissatisfaction—and boredom.

Information overload challenges the faith of classic liberalism that ever larger amounts of information—however noisy, trivial, and banal—processed, packaged and computerized—add up to progress. Information overload brings us to a point unimaginable to the classic liberal mind (J.S. Mill): that there could be too much information of any kind, good or bad. There was no place in Mill's theory for the possibility that one could have too much information. But information overload is such a possibility—especially when information is degraded into noise or banality.

Such a picture of overload dismisses the notion common among urbanites that boredom is mostly a problem of small towns, rural backwaters, or traditional societies outside the mainstream of progress. For all the allure of bright lights, the city has its own sorts of boredom. There is no evidence that people yawn more in small communities than in big ones.

By noting the busy boredom of high information load and large cities, the book does criticize our idea of progress. What can progress be if it does not banish boredom? And what can it be, if our institutions of entertainment, education, and maybe religion are serving as social placebos to stabilize a system that, behind the yawn, has a deep gap of meaning?

Maybe, however, such criticism—and especially understanding the relation of boredom to entropy as loss of potential—are the first necessary steps toward finding out what true progress is all about.

My field is sociology, but I have drawn material from diverse areas, such as psychology, communication studies, information science, economics, and imaginative literature for its insight. All the thoughts are tentative and require further research.

2

THE APPETITE FOR INFORMATION

As they rattled off down the road... the boys, round-eyed with excitement, studied every house and barn with such prolonged interest that their heads revolved on their necks like those of young owls.... Rock River had only one street of stores, blacksmith shops and taverns, but it was an imposing place to Lincoln.... When Lincoln spoke he whispered, as if in church, pointing with stubby finger, "See there!" each time some new wonder broke on his sight.... The buying of boots was the crowning joy of the day.... Then there were books to be bought, also, a geography, a "Ray's Arithmetic," and a slate.... At last, with all their treasures under the seat, where they could look at them or feel of them, with their slates clutched in their hands, the boys jolted toward home in silence.... Lincoln was pensive and silent all the evening, for he was busily digesting the mass of sights, sounds, and sensations which the day's outing had thrust upon him.

—From Hamlin Garland's *Boy Life on the Prairie* (1899)

This passage tells how it was in rural America before our transition to a media system, how thrilling were the simple sights and sounds of a small town to a boy who had no notion of movies, television, cassettes, radio; and, for that matter, little experience of telegraph and telephone. His world was quite as interesting to him, it seems, as ours is to us, though not so loaded with sensations.

Today his counterpart might be staring idly at a television or computer screen, inured to sights a hundred times more sensational. The difference is not merely in amount of media communication but of appetite for information—between that of a society where consumer goods and information were scarce, and that of a society where consumer goods and information are abundant.

Historically, it was a momentous transition, portrayed by Daniel Lerner's classic study of modernization, *The Passing of Traditional Society* (1958). Over the world, it was a change in developing countries from an oral to a media communication system, as media awaken desires for economic goods, jobs, political participation, and literacy. The traditional village or tribal society, in its self-contained world of oral networks, gave way to an urban, cosmopolitan world, in which media reporting global events replace chat and gossip with neighbors, and people are psychologically mobilized to aspire to new statuses and qualities of life. In such a development, information is highly prized as a means to such benefits; developing peoples eagerly grasp input from transistor radios, cinemas, newspapers, and television where available, perhaps after an ox cart brought the first transistor radio to their village, or they gathered around a television or movie projector powered by a generator.

As the total amount of media communication increases, the average person becomes exposed to much more exogenous information, from news, print, schooling, experts, fiction, drama, advertising, tourism, and so on. Not only does the amount increase but also the quality of communication changes, as Lerner (1958:55) described it, from personal and face-to-face to broadcast (mediated); primary group to heterogeneous mass; prescriptive (rules) to descriptive (news); and hierarchical (status) to professional (skill).

In such ways a media system delivers far more and different information, from strangers outside, than does an oral system, from members inside. Soon it becomes a system in which life is geared to media—in which people literally get up and go to bed by media; they are media-oriented: plugged into telephone, television, radio, cassettes, computers, film, credit-card transactions, and all the rest most of the time, on the job, in their cars, on the way to and from work, and at home. They hustle to keep up with information. Media orientation becomes a dependency that some experts do not hesitate to call addiction.

In such a context, it does not take long for media people to become aware of information overload, and to be unsure whether additional amounts of information make them all that better off.

Social scientists discovered that it was possible to have an overload of information. One of the first to notice it was the turn-of-the-century sociologist Georg Simmel (1950:415), who wrote of the attitude of reserve by which city people shield themselves from "indiscriminate suggestibility." He wrote of the overload of sensations in the urban world, causing city dwellers to become jaded and develop a kind of psychic callus, the blasé attitude, "an incapacity... to react to new situations with the appropriate energy" (pp. 410, 414). James G. Miller (1960) reported pioneering experiments in information overload of individuals and groups. Karl Deutsch (1961) noted that "communication overload" was a "disease of cities," in which freedom of choice is jammed by the very efficiency of communication and transport; so many things call for attention that people lack time to attend to anything or anyone. Richard Meier (1962:132) theorized broadly about information overload in cities, calculating that dwellers in modern cities, like San Francisco, bore 100 times the load of dwellers in less modern ones such as Addis Ababa, Jakarta, or Tehran; and predicted a saturation in communications flow and crisis of overload within the next half century. Lucien Pye (1963:126) noted in developing countries an unselective hunger or eagerness for media, whereas the West was "nearly saturated," requiring people, "as a means of self-defense" to "develop the capacity to ignore much and to become selective." A psychiatrist (Meerloo, 1967) commented that the media "have become ensnarled in a gigantic traffic jam," whose overloading had caused a breakdown in some patients' communication systems. By 1970 Alvin Toffler characterized the crisis from information overload as "future shock."

And now we have an information society. The United States has become an information economy in the sense that over half of its gross national product (GNP) is transfer of information rather than material goods (Ferris, 1978), and over half its workers are in the field of information rather than service, industry, or agriculture (Porat, 1977; 1978:72; Machlup, 1980; Masuda, 1981; Cornish, 1982; Dizard, 1982). That a flood of information is upon us we need hardly to be reminded. Media collect news, telescopes scan space, electron microscopes reveal the smallest secrets, computers process data, an ever larger funnel gathers information to pour upon us. To mention just a few facts and figures: the amount of scientific information is doubling every six years (Stanford, 1971); the number of technical journals published in the world exceeds 100,000. Some 50,000 books were published in 1984, according to estimate of the American Association of Publishers (Hutshing, 1985). More than 30,000 go out of print each year. From the government alone, in 1977, came 70,000 new technical publications, and the Federal Register (a compilation of government regulations and notices) ran to 66,958 pages. Electronic data processors can transmit about 256,000 bits of information each second. Professionals cannot keep up in their fields though they read as much as they can. Xeroxing multiplies copies needing to be read; libraries are submerged by the "paper flood"; the Postal Service loads mailboxes with junk mail. Media not only report news but overkill it by repetition and trivial detail, by which news magazines and newsletters reciprocally boost circulation by "dressing up" what newspapers have already said (Manning, 1968:158–159).

Along with all this information came a less comfortable feeling that it was not making more sense—even with help of computers—than it had before. The modern world was in a crisis of meaning, that one need only mention names like Kafka, Sartre, Beckett, and Eliot to demonstrate. The crisis has been called by many names—alienation, existential despair, absurdity, disenchantment, legitimation crisis, identity problem, anomie, sensate culture, counterculture, future shock, end of ideology, false consciousness, to mention a few. T.S. Eliot linked this crisis with information when he asked in "The Rock," where is the wisdom lost in knowledge and where is the knowledge lost in information?

In a crisis of meaning, amidst all the facts, one finds little by way of conviction that is reliable to hang onto. Traditions are discarded, institutions—even the most hallowed—are weakly legitimated and justify themselves by rhetoric regarded by many as boring or hypocritical. All one seems to find, as T.S. Eliot wrote in "The Wasteland," is a "heap of broken images." In lieu of reliable images, interpretations become impromptu, relativistic (McHugh, 1968:99, 107, 121, 136), and temporary; that is, interpretation of an event is not a matter of what is so but what one can "carry off" rhetorically and dramatically with a given audience (Becker, 1962:117–121). One sign of meaning gap is a flood of cultic movements, within and outside conventional churches, groping for meaning, as seekers shop from guru to guru for something to believe in or a glimpse of reality beyond ordinary consciousness. Nor can one ignore millions of people turning to magic, horoscopes, divination, *I Ching*, and so on, for interpretation of what is happening or about to happen. In this crisis of meaning, the contemporary rush to personal computers seems a last desperate attempt to master the tidal wave of incoming information. Since the crisis has occurred in the midst of a flood of information about which people do not know quite what to think, there seems little reason to be confident that further increases in public information—whether from science, or news agencies, or publishing, or education, or official pronouncements—will restore a meaning that seems to be slipping away. Indeed, the realization that science, especially its ideology scientism, is not providing answers to the question of human meaning is itself part of the crisis.

With such developments, it is understandable that the modern appetite for information is hardly one of unalloyed eagerness. Still less is it the reverence of Abraham Lincoln toward the books from which he got his education (contrasting with the modern college student's attitude toward textbooks).

To be sure, the modern appetite is voracious to the point of gluttony as people strive to consume media output and stay abreast. But the appetite, however huge, is tinged with contrary elements. First is satiety, a certain queasiness from overeating instead of the comfort of one who has dined well. The public palate is also jaded or blasé—desensitized to what would have shocked the previous generation.

Third, there is a distinct thread of resentment of such things as television commercials, sex and violence content, and incessant ringing of telephones. More people than one might realize have become nonanswerers to the telephone. They let it ring, cut off the ring, or record calls on an answering device. This is far from the enthusiasm of the community that listened in on the rural party line. There is also a defensive attitude, of fending off unwanted information. For the bulk of information, though some is momentarily useful, there is indifference or disdain, a throwaway attitude toward paperwork, magazines, and even books.

Finally, people are continually on the verge of boredom because so much information is irrelevant, meaningless, or trivial—or urgent but they can do nothing about it. We see boredom as having a defensive function as a barrier against noise.

What such negative elements in the appetite for information suggest is that along with the growth of information there has been a decline in its marginal value or meaning. The point might be made with the economist's idea of marginal utility. Yet another useful economic analogy is that the decline of value of information was rather like an inflation of currency: the more there was of it, the less it seemed to "buy" in meaning.

What the information society of the late twentieth century demonstrated is that information is not necessarily an answer. It, too, is a problem, like everything else.

3

WHERE IS BOREDOM?

Boredom is but one thread in the tangled skein of whatever may be wrong with modern life; but I think it tells of loss of meaning from overloads of information that are dysfunctional either because of too much redundancy or too much noise, as will be examined in following chapters. However, here we are concerned with the prevalence of boredom—how widespread is it, where does it occur, does it deserve to be regarded as a societal symptom?

Some people say they are never bored. They like their jobs. They have interesting hobbies. They are good conversationalists. They have firm faith in the meaning of it all. Their fertile imaginations divert them even in solitary confinement. They escape adroitly from situations that threaten to trap them in trivia. They begrudge themselves barely six hours of sleep. There is little reason to believe that such people are bored.

But others readily admit being bored much of the time, not just in work but in leisure and voluntary activities. I call to mind a man who says he carries a book wherever he goes, to avoid boredom while waiting or riding. Or take a married couple, of which the husband is engrossed in a career and hobbies that take him away much from home. But the wife readily admits she is bored and yawns a lot.

Plainly this is a problem that strikes individuals in different ways. Some people are trapped in boring jobs or situations. Some boredom may be in the eye of the beholder. Some is due to a social structure or culture that affects many, though participation varies. Let us consider signs that boredom is not just a personal idiosyncrasy but a considerable social problem affecting many people in sectors beyond that of work.

A strange cloud hangs over modern life. At first it was not noticed; now it is thicker than ever. It embarrasses claims that the quality of life is getting better. It reduces commitment to work. It is thickest in cities where there are the most varieties, pleasures, and opportunities. Like smog, it spreads to all sorts of places it is not supposed to be.

The most common name for this cloud is boredom. And the most common mistake is to think of it as occurring only in monotonous work and the long traffic-jammed rides to and from it. To be sure, work is much to blame. Phrases like "assembly-line blues," "paper shuffling," "Thank God, it's Friday," "Tuesday-through-Thursday syndrome" (absenteeism before or after weekends), "blue collar revolt" express widespread recognition of boredom in work. National magazines periodically run stories with captions like, "Bored on the Job" (*Life*), or "Boredom Epidemic—Illness of the Age" (*National Observer*, May 13, 1972). Work is described in terms like the following: "The women may not even know what they are assembling or who will use it. They are bored. They lift their eyes only to watch the clock. When break time comes there's a sudden mass exit." The president of a car rental firm writes, "The boys in the mail room, the presidents, and the girls in the steno pool have three things in common: they are docile, they are bored, and they are dull." The manager of a company making refrigerators deplores the loss of motivation to work:

We're all bored with what we are doing. Students don't want to study; workers don't want to work. Managers don't want to manage; garbage collectors don't want to collect garbage. The question nowadays is "Who wants to do what they're supposed to do?"

Practically every survey of attitudes toward work reveals boredom, especially where jobs are monotonous, mechanized, and control is lacking over the whole task. A task force of the Department of Health, Education and Welfare (HEW) in 1972 issued a massive report on "Work in America," declaring that the American work force was becoming dissatisfied with dull, unchallenging, and repetitive jobs. Terkel (1973) noted among both white collar and blue-collar workers attitudes ranging from passive boredom to indignation at degradation and dehumanization. For example:

I stand in one spot, about two or three feet area, all night. We do about thirty-two jobs per car per unit, forty-eight units an hour, eight hours a day. Thirty-two times forty-eight times eight, figure it out. That's how many times I pushed that button (Terkel, 1973:221). Repetition is such that if you were to think about the job itself, you'd slowly go out of your mind. You'd let your problems build up, you get to the point where you'd be at the fellow next to you—his throat (Terkel, 1973:222).

A similar picture of boredom on the production line is given by Garson (1975).

A later survey (Quinn and Staines, 1978) sponsored by the U.S. Department of Labor, interviewing 1,500 workers, found that a growing number of Americans were dissatisfied with their jobs and believed that their "quality of life" was deteriorating. Although the majority still were satisfied (the happiest workers were the self-employed), there had been a significant decline in satisfaction since 1969 among blacks, semi-skilled, and blue-collar workers, workers under 30, and especially college graduates. Fewer workers felt that their work was interesting; more than one-third believed that their skills were not fully utilized; and almost as many said their education exceeded their job requirements. More workers also felt "locked in" on their jobs, with opportunities for mobility decreasing.

Seemingly discrepant with these findings is the report by Campbell (1981:42) that when American workers were asked how satisfied they were with the work they were doing, four out of five said they were at least moderately satisfied; and when asked if they would want to continue to work if they were to come into enough money "to live as comfortably as you would like for the rest of your life," the large majority said they would. But it is important to distinguish boredom from dissatisfaction with work. There are many reasons to be satisfied with a job regardless of the fact that it is boring; indeed, adjustment to work may include *acceptance* of boredom. Many people feel that work gives more personal significance than does leisure, even though the former may be more boring.

There is also the problem of under-reporting of boredom, discussed later in this chapter. Unrecognized and unreported boredom is a main point of the romantic criticism of society: the philistine satisfied with his existence does not know how bored he is and how alive he could be. Campbell admits that there may be "some element of 'false consciousness'" in job satisfaction (1981:42).

Boredom was found to be one cause of "assembly-line hysteria" by a study with a data base of about a thousand cases (Colligan and Stockton, 1978). The most monotonous jobs, lowest in the pecking order and often high in stress, are the most boring. It is a mistake to think of stress as an antidote for boredom, for undemanding, boring roles often cause more stress than do demanding ones (Palmer, 1981:95–99). Robert Kaplan (1975) in a study of 23 occupations found that the three most undemanding and boring occupations were assembly-line work, machine tending, and operating a fork lift. In these jobs workers experienced more psychosomatic complaints and depression than workers in other jobs.

On up the hierarchy things are not all that much better. Even among young executives at middle management levels, a "creeping death" was reported. An editor of a trade journal commented: "Boredom has crept from the assembly line all the way up to the executive suite." Firms launched anti-boredom campaigns, hiring experts, trying job enrichment, job rotation, group assembly, and other ways, but many confessed a losing battle: that there was no ultimate escape from the tedium of the machine—especially the human machine called bureaucracy.

It is all too easy to blame work for modern boredom, but flogging that horse will carry us only so far. Other sectors have their share of boredom.

To youth, though not yet employed, the phrase, "nine-to-five" has come to be a symbol of boring existence. It is understandable that school could help instill this feeling. Sociologist Robert Sommer (1969:98) writes:

Most schools are still boxes filled with cubes each containing a specified number of chairs in straight rows. . . . Everywhere one looks there are "lines." The straight rows tell the student to look ahead and ignore everyone except the teacher.

The picture of high schools is hardly reassuring. One superintendent ruefully admitted of his own school, "All they get is lousy busy work. It's horrible. They're just putting in time." Viewing the educational scene, Charles E. Silberman (1970) said, "The banality and triviality of the curriculum in most schools has to be experienced to be believed." For a voice from the ranks, read this letter from a 17-year-old girl in Los Angeles:

Hi Verna: What are you doing? *I'm so bored* I can't stand it. I'm in study hall right now. . . . Our study hall teacher is Miss S. She's a twenty-five year old maid who wears her hair in a bun and wears dresses down to her knees. Every time we talk, we get a "demerit" and three demerits mean we have to go to the headmaster's office. I have 26 demerits as of October 6. School is beginning to get to me. There's this girl named Alison. . . . Today during sports, a friend of mine Ruth and I sprayed her with a hose and locked her out of the History room where we had to sand the desks. It was so fun, she really got mad, and I hope took the hint. Other boring things around school are: I'm flunking Biology (I got a 60 on my last report card and I'm doing worse). . . . Also, I got in trouble for writing notes in English. As I say, I am getting fed up. During sports every day we ride to town (by bicycle) and buy things. Lately, we've been buying cinnamon rolls and pie. We smuggle them back to school to eat them. But even this is boring. I think maybe I'll take tennis or volleyball. . . . A lot of people are becoming Jesus Freaks. The bell just rang and school is over, thank God, except it's just as boring at home. I don't know which I hate more, home or school. School is such a drag. . . .

Larkin (1979:129) reports on the boredom of suburban youth at "Utopia High":

Boredom is the universal element that transcends all social divisions. . . . Throughout the study, the theme of boredom recurred. For the active students, engrossing themselves in projects and events provided a bulwark against it. For the more passive, it has become a way of life. Boredom hung over Utopia like a thick fog. It was something everyone had to cope with: a fact of life even for those who chose to avoid it. Several students led frenetic lives in which they ran from one activity to the next so they would not succumb to boredom. However, most gave into it. . . . Many students ditched classes and hung out on the premises . . . "goofing off." When asked what their lives were like, they unanimously stated that they were boring.

At a suburban high school in Chicago, interviews with 75 seniors from the top 5 percent showed that the affluent high school experience is a deadly boring process which must be endured (Linton and Pollack, 1978).

If a student imagines that when he gets to college things will be very different, he may be disappointed. Universities resound with complaints about "cram-and-regurgitate," endless lecturing, large classes, bureaucracy, degree factories. The following conversation, overheard on a bus, tells much of university students' attitudes toward studies: "What did you get?"—"Oh, a B."—"What was the course about?"—"I can't remember."—"What book did you use?"—"Somebody's."—"Who was the teacher?"—"That's too long ago. Ha, ha." Students complained about lack of involvement in educational decisions; but, after they were given the right to sit on faculty committees, found them so boring it became difficult to get a student to attend. As a dean at the University of Florida put it:

The longer one stays in school, the harder it is to get him to serve on a committee ... they have discovered that committees are a bore and they have discovered why deans send assistant deans to the meetings (New York Times Service, April 1, 1976).

An entire supplement to the *Santa Barbara News and Review* January 24, 1980, was entitled, "BORED."

Is home a haven from boredom? One should hope so, but there is plenty there, too. Housewives are no less restless in traditional roles of homemaking than are husbands at work and children at school. "Overall, women say they are about as satisfied with housework as all respondents (including men) who work for pay say they are with their paid jobs," but only one-fifth of college graduates say they are completely satisfied as contrasted with over half of those with less than a high school education (Campbell, Converse and Rodgers, 1976:306). Boredom of child raising is a consideration in some married couples' decisions to remain childless (Veevers, 1980:76). However, a majority of women like taking care of their home: in a poll by the Institute for Social Research in 1971, six out of ten said without reservation that they enjoyed taking care of their home (Campbell, 1981:132). Yet, entering business and industrial careers, perhaps they find only a different kind of boredom than they did at home. Do six and one-half hours of television-watching—soaps, kids' comics, sports, and violence—testify to no boredom or plenty of it (needing relief or compensation by entertainment, as discussed in Chapter 10)? Modern literature dwells on domestic boredom: "Spiteful domestic bickering arising from ennui sets the acrimonious tone of much modern literature, most notably in the theater of Chekhov, Sartre, Ionesco, and Albee" (Kuhn, 1976:274n).

Drug and alcohol abuse—on the job, in school, and for recreation—are commonly attributed in part to boredom, and I see no reason to doubt it. A sociological study of working-class youth (Schwartz et al., 1973) reports escape from boredom as a major motive for using pot to get stoned. Three girls working in Manhattan explain how pot relieves boredom:

We've got these stupid jobs, clerical jobs in a couple of brokerages. We either work our fool heads off, nights and Saturdays included, when they're busy, or they talk about laying off girls—us, because things are slack.... We've had it. What we do is come out here to relax. Two or three joints and we feel good. We don't care if it might be our last week on the job. We don't care if the work is stupid, we can stand it then. When we go back, it wears off after a while and we go down again, but we've had it. We've been up (Townsend, 1970).

A similar picture is given by military life, reflected by news captions like "GIs Fight Boredom," "Military Battles Liquor Bottle." A survey of naval recruits in 1977 showed that 46 percent had serious alcohol problems before they entered and estimated 55,000 alcoholics in the navy (10 percent of the total force). The Army General Accounting Office reported 20 percent of officers and 32 percent of enlisted men to be either "heavy" or "binge" drinkers. The American Defense Department estimated in 1970 that between 25 and 30 percent of all United States service personnel worldwide were at least experimenting with drugs other than alcohol, the commonest, marijuana, having been used by between 50 and 80 percent of all Army personnel in Vietnam at least once. (A notorious embarrassment came to the Navy in 1973, when, of an honor guard welcoming Soviet leader Leonid Brezhnev to Washington, 13 sailors had to be transferred for smoking pot; and, a month before, 12 working the president's yacht moved for the same reason.) In 1981 the Navy and Marine Corps came out with a new hard-line policy, calling for immediate discharge of officers and top enlisted personnel using drugs and authorizing searching mail for contraband, urinalysis to detect abusers, and dogs to sniff out drugs. Recognizing the connection with boredom, the commandant of the Marine Corps asked base commanders to provide video game centers and first-run movies on base to keep Marines away from places where they might meet drug dealers (Cooper, 1981).

By the early 1980s cocaine abuse took center stage as a serious problem among well-off, successful people—the typical user being white, male, professional, and upper-middle-class. Deaths from mixing alcohol and cocaine drew widespread attention to the problem. "Cocaine usage has become epidemic," said Dr. Jack Durell, deputy director of the National Institute of Drug Abuse, figures released by that agency showing a fivefold increase in users seeking help in treatment programs between

1975 and 1980 (*San Diego Union*, March 14, 1982). Because cocaine is a stimulant that makes users feel happy, powerful, self-confident, energetic, and sexually aroused, it seems reasonable that it would especially appeal to those who are bored and want to live more intensely.

Institutional religion is another place where one expects to encounter tedium, if only from archaic and repetitious ritual, doctrinal platitudes, and long sits on hard pews. Such an atmosphere is evoked by Christoper Morley saying of a certain cleric: "Even in the church, where boredom is prolific, I hail thee first, Episcopalian bore: Who else could serve as social soporific and without snoring teach the rest to snore." And Thomas Hardy says of Farmer Oak in *Far from the Madding Crowd*, "He went to church, but yawned privately by the time the congregation reached the Nicene Creed, and thought of what there would be for dinner when he meant to be listening to the sermon." Boredom is the acknowledged enemy of meditation. It is also true of the urban church that a crowd of utter strangers is not as interesting as a congregation well known to one another. So there is plenty of boredom in institutional religion. The rapid growth of theatrical evangelism and the "electronic church" testifies to an effort to overcome what Pentecostals call "ho hum" religion. So does the boom of exotic cults during the 1960s and 1970s, a movement of seekers "shopping" for gurus, rituals, revelations, or highs by which to give new meaning to life (Klapp, 1969). How many seekers are there? No one knows exactly; but during the 1970s there were an estimated 10 million Americans using horoscopes and following astrology; a boom of sales of religious and inspirational books; and, according to Gallup (1976), 12 percent of Americans practicing meditation or actively involved in other sorts of mysticism. It was as though people were peering into inner or outer space to find a new dimension.

Politics also struggles against boredom much of the time, with the public attitude toward it and its rhetoric usually described as apathetic, except when momentarily aroused by crises, special issues, or scandals. Voter turnout in America is notoriously low, often less than 50 percent (the 1974 vote for U.S. representatives fell to a shocking 36.2 percent). Legislative proceedings get low television ratings. Political party conventions, for all their fanfare, are usually, as described by one news writer, an "enormous tedium," failing to hold the interest of television audiences as well as do sports, quiz shows, and giveaway games. Even for what is frankly entertainment, high turnover and short life of television shows with declining Nielsen ratings show that audiences are hard to please and quickly bored. Passivity—sitting back and watching without taking part—is a large reason for the boredom of audiences. Britain, too, recognizes a problem of public apathy in voting; but Martin (1961:89–91) argued that it is the political cousin of consumer resistance—both having "positive value" for democracy as an antidote to conformism and high-pressure salesmanship.

Boredom even creeps into talk and sociability—the chat of the cocktail party and gossip around the coffee machine. Clichés bring yawns. That the problem is not trivial is suggested by a widely printed advertisement for a course in conversational improvement, which asks ARE YOU A BORE? and offers to remedy the lack by correspondence lessons. In similar helpful vein, a newspaper article outlines tactics for getting rid of bores: "Smile and greet, but keep moving," talk about oneself until the bore backs away, offer to get the bore a drink before excusing oneself, introduce the bore to someone else, see someone with whom one must have a few words, depart to take care of one's contact lenses, help the hostess (Nemy, 1980). Such tactics make one wonder if everybody is avoiding everybody. They also lead one to ask if boredom has gotten so prevalent that people have to be *instructed* in how to talk to one another. Wits have their fun. Hilaire Belloc (1931) describes with sly humor the art of boring people in conversation. Voltaire said, "The secret of being a bore is to tell everything." It is easy to attribute some of the boredom of conversation to lack of communal concerns of a rootless society. Clichés become the standard currency, because they are the easiest and safest form of communication, and the likelihood is small that chat will be about anything in which all parties are personally interested. André Gregory, director of the film, "My Dinner with André," said that one of the initial impulses for making this acclaimed movie was that

Wally and I were struck by the fact that we found that nobody talked about anything anymore that came from the heart, that was felt. We sensed that most conversation had become automatic.... And that there was no real communication going on.... Social intercourse becomes deadly and boring and unlife-enhancing (*Christian Science Monitor*, February 7, 1983).

How widespread is conscious boredom in America? It is not easy to tell from polls that have been taken. A Gallup poll of October 9, 1969 (the last taken on the question, "Do you find life exciting—or dull?")

found that half of U.S. adults answered "dull" or "pretty routine." A 51-year-old woman typist said: "I find life monotonous with never any change. I go to work, come home, go to bed, get up and go to work. I'm alone now—I've raised my son—I guess I'm in a rut." On the other hand, from the half of the sample who said "exciting," a 34-year-old wife of an Indianapolis executive said: "Anyone who finds life dull is either half dead or sound asleep. He should look around, move around, talk with people. The world is full of excitement." Half of adults are a lot of people to be bored in a society as diverted by news and entertainment as ours is. A more favorable picture is reported by Andrews and Withey (1976:321): 30 percent of Americans remembered that they had been bored more than once in the past few weeks. A higher proportion is reported by Campbell (1981:239) in answer to the same question ("During the past few weeks have you ever felt bored?"): about one-third answered yes (1965, 34 percent; 1972, 37 percent; 1978, 30 percent). In another poll (Campbell, Converse, and Rodgers, 1976:38) a lower proportion was found: of 2,151 respondents asked to rate their lives on a seven-point scale from very boring to very interesting, 18 percent fell in the boring half of the scale whereas 82 percent fell in the interesting half.

From such variation, it is safe to say that we know too little about what proportion of the population is bored; and what kinds of people they are; and how deep or chronic various sorts of boredom (from tedium to ennui) are; and how it is related to social status, education, work, religion, life-style, mental health, age, and so on.

And we must ask, if 50 or only 30 or even only 18 percent are consciously bored, how many more are unconsciously so or unwilling to report? There are at least three reasons why an opinion poll may be expected to under-report boredom. One is that a person may not be skilled in characterizing—even have a name for—his own psychological state; he can be bored, depressed, resentful, prejudiced, and so on, without ever having called it that, still less report feelings that are unconscious in a Freudian sense. Second, more than temporary boredom is commonly considered a fault; so people are not eager to characterize their work, home life, church, entertainment, and so on in such terms— even if it is true and they know it. Third, placebo institutions such as entertainment, gambling, sports, drugs, and media may be palliating or masking boredom so that people do not realize their own hidden hungers (see Chapter 10)—further reason for saying that they do not really know what the level of boredom is. Under-reporting negative affect was noted by Andrews and Withey (1976:332–333): "From our data... people tend to see their own lives as better than most other people's lives.... Optimism is another apparent phenomenon that keeps people from assimilating some of the sting of current conditions." Campbell (1981:50) also comments on the tendency to under-report negative aspects of one's own life:

We have seen how reluctant Americans are to describe themselves as "not too happy" or not satisfied with life.... When they talk about the specific areas of their lives they are much more likely to be positive than negative. This cannot be attributed to a characteristic American tendency.... Similar distributions, although not quite so positive, are reported when Europeans are asked similar questions.

To be sure, there are situations where people could be expected to *over*-report boredom, such as where it is a fashionable pose, as in aristocratic disdain.

Is the picture so different in other advanced countries? In Sweden, all accounts agree that, along with the benefits of the welfare state, boredom is notoriously high, reflected in gambling, alcoholism, and suicide.

In France, boredom was widely blamed for the university student rebellion of 1968—"*La France S'Ennui*," said *Le Monde* (Seeman, 1972). A huge literature dwells on the theme of ennui.

From Japan come reports of the "dull, workaholic atmosphere of Japanese society," producing a surge of adventurism and thrill-seeking among the young. A Japanese polar explorer explains, "I think many young Japanese feel frustrated at the lack of challenge in society today. They have been spoon-fed in childhood, and once they become adults they are locked into a dull working routine that offers them little freedom" (Murray, 1980).

In Britain, as in the United States, "boredom" is conspicuous among the slogans of the "punk rock" movement expressing frustrations of pent-up youth, by torn T-shirts, cigarette burns, safety pins (in the fabric and through the ears), swastikas, and other such symbols aiming to shock. A concessioner at Brighton, England, noting the boredom that has descended on that once popular beach resort, attributed it to raised expectations.

People are so much more intelligent than years ago. They watched television, they traveled, and they learned to get bored. How many days a year can you walk around the Brighton seafront with your shirt off and a bag of chips in your hand? It's got limits. There's not an 18-year-old kid alive in Britain now who doesn't have bigger expectations (Vinocur, 1979).

A British radio station took a poll to determine the most boring town in England. The vote went to Grantham in Lincolnshire which happens to be the hometown of Prime Minister Margaret Thatcher. After the award, the George Hotel on Grantham's High Street did not waste a moment but announced "the world's most boring tour" to go with the town's new title. With tongue-in-cheek, they suggested that a car tour to nearby villages might relieve the boredom, but only after listening to a required lecture on Thatcher's early life (Morgan, 1981).

Switzerland, regarded by many as a model country, gives a sharp picture of boredom affecting youth who were thought to have "everything." In Zurich in October 1980 a riot over the closing of a youth center "crept across Switzerland, feeding on the restlessness of a young generation anxious to break out of a suffocating society." Banners and graffiti in Lausanne proclaimed: "We don't want a world where the guarantee of not dying from hunger is paid for by the certainty of dying from boredom." A young man explained, "We have everything—stereo, television, food, a place to sleep, everything. Our parents say, 'Here's some money, now go away.' We want something else." Lausanne's director of police commented:

There is a certain malaise which is directly linked to our prosperity.... There is no longer any need to struggle for survival. It's enough to get by, to have a job and time to go sailing and to the mountains. We have all we need.... The young people of this country don't like what they see of the adult world: no creativity, no imagination.

A youthful demonstrator explained, "All I want is someplace to go and have fun. There is nothing political involved at all. I'm just bored." Pointing to a clock with moving soldiers and dancers," he said, "That's Switzerland for you right there. Mechanical, cute and programmed. Only the clothes change" (Carmel, 1980).

Nor does particular content of ideology appear to have much to do with the prevalence of boredom (unless it were from taking any ideology too seriously). In the Soviet Union, for example, following is a typical picture of youth given in the media: "Bored, listless, and avoiding state-provided clubrooms, teenagers across the country offend and alarm parents and adults by gathering after school, drinking wine, smoking, and preening themselves in Western fashions" (Willis, 1978). A Soviet youth journal said, " 'I do not know why I am so bored,' says a young girl. 'We live as in a desert.' 'How to pass one's time?' asks a young man. 'One is bored.' Generally boredom ends in a drinking bout (Wohl, 1976).

From such glimpses and surveys we have, then, a picture of sectors of modern societies in which boredom is a familiar problem. Worthy activities with which one can find no logical fault are nevertheless boring.

Perhaps this explains why so many words refer to boredom. The following list may suggest that there is more boredom than people recognize by that particular name: accidie (acedia), anhedonia, apathy, arid, banal, banality, blasé, burn-out, chatter, chatterbox, glazed eyes, hackneyed, harping, ho hum, humdrum, inane, insipid, insouciance, repetitious, routine, rut, sameness, satiety, soporific, stagnant, stagnation, sterile, chitchat, chore, cliché, cloying, dismal, doldrums, drag, dreary, dry, dull, dullness, effete, enervation, ennui, flat, irksome, jade, jaded, jejune, languor, lassitude, listless, long-winded, monotony, museum fatigue, pall, platitude, prolixity, prosaic, prosy, stuffy, stupefying, surfeited, tedium, tedious, tiresome, torpor, trite, trivia, uninteresting, verbosity, weariness, wearisome, world-weary.

Some of these distinctions, as between boredom and ennui, and kindred states (such as satiation, habituation, and jading), will be pursued later in this chapter and the next. Right now, we merely note how many words for, and how many nuances of, boredom there are. Do we need them all to describe various situations in modern life? That we have so many words plausibly suggests that modern people have need for them just as the Eskimo has so many words for snow. Showing not only the prevalence of boredom but its various dimensions and kindred states, these words help us to conceive it better as a social and psychological problem.

Perhaps it is revealing that the words boredom, monotony, and routine came into more use in America from 1931 to 1961. Word counts for those years showed that these three words together became two and a half times more common in 1961 than in 1931—and boredom by itself perhaps 10 times more common.[1] It seems reasonable to infer that if people wrote more about boredom, presumably there was more. At least there is no suggestion that boredom was waning.

The theme of boredom is copiously reflected in modern literature. The term *bore* apparently came into literary use during the eighteenth century ("cannot be traced before the 1760s"—Peters, 1975). The words, boredom and, bore were not in the first edition of Samuel Johnson's *Dictionary of the English Language*, (1755). The first use recorded by the *Oxford English Dictionary* was a complaint by a writer (Evelyn, 1667) that, "We have hardly any words that do fully express the French naivete, ennui, bizarre, etc." By 1732, Berkeley was remarking that people "prefer doing anything to the *ennui* of their own conversation." Lord Chesterfield reported in 1758 that "living like a gentleman was dying of ennui." By 1826 *ennui* had become part of the title of a book, *Diary of an Ennuyee* by Jamison. Darwin even got around to finding it in animals: "Animals manifestly . . . suffer from ennui" (1871). On the whole, the term boredom came into fashion in English literature after ennui did. Of stylish living, W.E. Forster (1847) wrote, "We drove to a first-class hotel . . . a stylish, comfortless temple of ennui," and of fashionable dress, Charlotte Bronte (1849) wrote, "Every stitch she put on was an ennui." Dickens in *Bleak House* (1952) diagnosed a "chronic malady of boredom." George Elliot described the gentleman as a man "whose grace of bearing has been moulded on an experience of boredom" (1876), who could "assert his superiority and show a more vigorous boredom" (1879). Boredom was ascribed to a social class: "the class of bores as a whole" (1883), "boredom rejoiced—gossip clapped her hand" (1883). Lord Byron's statement is especially significant: "Society is now one polished horde,/Formed of two mighty tribes,/the Boring and the/Bored" (*Juan*, 1823).

Judging by such writings, it seems that in England boredom came into vogue during the eighteenth century first by importing the French word, *ennui*, then became widely recognized as a social problem during the nineteenth century. This eruption into consciousness was perhapos paralleled in Russia: "It's a new fashion they have invented, being bored; in old days no one was bored" (Nicolai Gogol, *Dead Souls*, 1842; New York: Modern Library, 1936, p. 148).

By the twentieth century, says Kuhn's (1976) comprehensive study of ennui in literature, it is "not one theme among others; it is the dominant theme" (p.331)—"a modern plague" (p. 375). Ennui is distinguished from ordinary boredom by being deeper, chronic, a feeling of meaninglessness or spiritual anguish. It is a major theme for a huge number of writers, including Pascal, Schopenhauer, Voltaire ("Candide"), Samuel Johnson ("Rasselas"), Rousseau, Goethe, Flaubert, Beckett, Sartre, T.S. Eliot, Corneille, La Rochefoucauld, Baudelaire, Sterne, Balzac, Leopardi, Coleridge, Stendhal, Huysmans, DeMaupassant, Kierkegaard, Hemingway, Kafka, Moravia, Mann, Camus, Checkhov, and Proust.

As portrayed in literature (however it may be in the world of work), most ennui occurs among people who are idle and rich, often aristocrats, as George Eliot describes them: "Good society has its claret and its velvet carpets, it dinner engagements six weeks deep, its opera and its fairy ballrooms; rides off its ennui on thoroughbred horse" (*The Mill on the Floss*). Having "everything" in terms of status and wealth, they yet feel empty, as portrayed in plays by John Osborne:

People who have achieved everything except their hearts' desires. They are caught in the joyless round of choosing the top hotel to stay at, the finest restaurant to dine in, the most delectable partner to sleep with. Boredom infects their days and nights, and drink is their anodyne. (As described by *Time*, August 9, 1968)

Much of this emptiness come from satiety. So as an American heiress (Anne Bernays, 1975) described her "marzipan life," it was "simply the way I was brought up . . . to me it was the same old dreary thing: day after day of marzipan, silk velvet, Steuben glass, butterballs." Of course, falls from polo ponies and crashes of fast cars can help offset aristocratic ennui. But seeking stronger sensations produces jading (desensitization), a vicious circle in which indulgence leads to ever-larger requirements of stimulation. Such a picture is found in Balzac's *The Fatal Skin*, in which the gambler and sensualist plunge into ever-greater excess, though he knows it is at cost of his own life.

Lack of significant work adds to a sense of uselessness. In Chekhov's play "Three Sisters" Baron Lieutenant Tusenbach complains of "the laziness, the contempt for work, the rotten boredom afflicting our society"; Colonel Vershinin announces, "It's the same old thing! My wife has attempted suicide again"; and the last line of the play is, "If only we knew [what life is for]." Perhaps it was the thought of such ennui that led Baudelaire to remark, "Everything considered, work is less boring than amusing oneself."

It should be noted that some of the ennui of aristocrats is not so much a feeling as affectation, a pose of hauteur and disdain for work and other activities of the common person—a status-maintaining device.

The ennui of the common person has recieved less attention than that of the aristocrat; but common people, too, have their share. In views like those of Pascal, Voltaire ("Candide"), Schopenhauer, and Beckett, it is a universal human predicament. One sees it in the two old tramps in Beckett's "Waiting for Godot," talking trivia ("We are bored to death"), waiting for the Big Answer that never comes. The garden variety of ordinary boredom is illustrated by a lithograph by Honoré Daumier, "Six mois de mariage" (1869) showing a married couple sitting together in their living room, both yawning. Benjamin Franklin, in *Poor Richard's Almanac* (1733), wrote, "After three days men grow weary of a wench, a guest, and rainy weather." Logan Pearsall Smith adds, "What a bore it is waking up with the same person."

At its deepest, however, ennui is more than ordinary boredom, a malaise of meaning that infects the very roots of existence. It might be world-weariness such as that of Faust, who has run the gamut of experience and knowledge, "had it all," and found it empty. As portrayed in the Italian film, "La Dolce Vita," ennui is a symptom of nihilism, despair, and decadence. In Huysmans's *Against the Grain*, the hero, Des Esseintes, is so paralyzed by ennui that he cannot even muster the will to complete a journey from Paris to London, longed for all his life. Unlike ordinary boredom, ennui is often inescapable—in Sartre's "No Exit," a hell in which selfish people are confined to live together for eternity.

There seems little doubt, from such portrayals and our list of synonyms, that boredom is a major social problem and not merely a trivial and temporary discomfort of a few individuals. We note an interesting connection of romanticism, boredom, and suicide in literary characters such as Flaubert's Emma Bovary, Ibsen's Hedda Gabler, Goethe's Werther, and Tolstoy's Anna Karenina. In such stories, a romantic person demands more of life than a dull predicament can afford, gets into deepening trouble, and then takes self-destruction as a way out. Perhaps it was this propensity to trouble that led Maupassant to remark, "A romantic in the house is like a rat in the corn crib."

Romantics deserve some credit for discovering boredom as a social problem. The contribution of romantic sensibility to the discovery of the social problem of boredom seems to have been considerable. Whether as writers or as fictional characters, they demanded that life be interesting and fulfilling. Holding up the ideal of a free and natural life, they attacked anything in society that stood in the way of self-expression—conventionality, parochialism, philistinism,[2] class privilege, machines, bureaucracy, "dark Satanic mills" (Blake), "cash nexus" (Carlyle), taxes (Thoreau), prudential marriage,[3] comfortable middle-class living,[4] even society itself (Rousseau). Doing so, they shifted blame for boredom and ennui from the lazy or rebellious individual to society, turning a fault of an individual into a reproach against a social order whose rules are oppressive. Finding shortcomings in the present state of affairs, they quest in far-off places, yearn for other eras, advocate a simple natural life (Thoreau, Tolstoy, Rousseau), flout the opinion of Main Street (Carol Kennicott), hold up an absurdly high ideal (Quixote), or daydream of better things (Walter Mitty, Miniver Cheevy). In their own eyes, romantics are heroes struggling against wrong from which it is their duty to rescue themselves, their art, even society. For such service, for pointing to such things, romantics deserve credit for helping discover boredom as a social problem. Their special sensitivity—to nature, to ideals—enables them to perceive denials and distortions of culture that their ordinary contemporaries were blind to. Questing for personal fulfillment, they spoke for the legitimacy of protest against boredom—the right *not* to be bored. Such a contribution to sensing subtle social problems I would liken to the canary carried into coal mines to detect dangerous fumes before humans could smell them—a social indicator.

Sociologists I would expect are professionally inclined to agree with romantics that some features of society are at fault for much of the boredom today. By saying that boredom is a social problem, I mean not only that it affects a considerable number of people, but that some of its causes are systemic—structural, cultural, or communicational. So Max Weber—whom I would hardly call romantic—drew a melancholy picture of man as a cog in a human machine, caught in an iron cage of rules and routine, charisma defeated by bureaucracy, that fitted well with romantic protest coming from writers like Kafka or Hesse, or Charles Chaplin portraying absurdities of the assembly line in his film, "Modern Times."

But, aside from romantic heroism, there is also the well-recognized connection of boredom with troublemaking. This picture is supported by literature such as Byron's "Don Juan," Chekhov's "The Seagull" (a girl drowns herself after being jilted by her lover who seduced her out of boredom), Conrad's *Victory* (the bored blackguard persecuting the hero), or Ibsen's Hedda Gabler destroying others' lives out of what seems sheer whim. Common sense agrees that the devil finds work for idle hands. And so, to some extent, do sociologists, who find some connection of boredom with juvenile crime. A study of 1,255 delinquent boys, black and non-black, showed that boredom is associated with delinquency: "the more often the boy feels he has nothing he wishes to do, the more likely he is to commit delinquent acts. The relation, however, is relatively weak, with only those who often feel unoccupied being unusually likely to commit delinquent acts" (Hirschi, 1969:193).

Three groups of juveniles in Sydney, Australia—one from a low-delinquency area, one from a high-delinquency area, and one of offenders in a correctional institution—showed significant agreement in their perceptions that the four most important causes of delinquency were peer influence, thrill-seeking, desire to prove oneself, and boredom (Kraus, 1977). A psychological study of ninth to thirteenth grade students showed that those who score high on susceptibility to boredom are more likely to engage in deviant behavior at school (Wasson, 1981). Commonly attributed to boredom is vandalism—from toilet graffiti to arson—which costs public schools more than $100,000,000 a year. Studies indicate that rates of vandalism are highest in schools with high boredom among pupils; and that one-third of high school students in San Diego, California, are truant occasionally or frequently, with boring classes cited as the major reason. Bertrand Russell observed, "Boredom is a vital problem for the moralist, since at least half the sins of mankind are caused by fear of it" (*The Conquest of Happiness*, IV). It would be an irony of affluence if boredom with too much, not a lack of something, were found to be a major cause of crime.

Another significant connection, yet to be fully explored, is Eric Hoffer's (1951) observation that not material frustration but boredom of people escaping from drab, unfulfilled lives was at the root of fanatical social movements of the early twentieth century. So—from the prevalence of boredom in modern countries, its rich vocabulary, portrayal in literature, part in the protests of romantics, and connection with trouble-making we see that boredom is a serious social problem, not a trivial or transitory discontent that will blow away with a change of mood or of air.

Such signs of boredom in modern life put into an interesting light the fun industries going full blast, pouring entertainment and products on people, everything one could think of to make leisure more satisfying:

unending TV, film, stage shows; recording hits; sports spectacles; foods, beverages, fashions, gadgets; equipment for fishing, hunting, surfing, boating, water skiing, aqua lunging, gliding, flying; recreational vehicles (dune buggies, carpeted vans with hi-fi, campers, Land Rovers, bikes, scooters, Mopeds, snowmobiles); parks and national forests taking reservations from eager vacationers; jumbo jets carrying crowds of tourists wherever they want to go; advertisements urging "enjoy yourself," and inviting people with free air trips to pleasure domes like Las Vegas; instruction in hobbies from flower-arranging to Kung Fu and manuals on how to have fun—one describing 74 ways (Julius Fast, *The Pleasure Book*, 1975); Play-boy Clubs offering their Superkey (a credit card) as a talisman by which businessmen can "fight boredom in every Club city," while teenage pinball machine addicts play computer games with fantasy villains from outer space. Does so much equipment and pursuit of pleasure tell us that boredom is being defeated, or that it is a motive of such pursuit?

A similar question is raised about rapidly changing fads and fashions, so numerous in modern life. We see a parade of novelties—song hits, best sellers, new styles of clothing and furnishings, health foods, medicines, diets, and so on—which pique popular taste, then pass out of fashion. Would there be so many, and would they change so fast, were it not for boredom? That is, does boredom create an appetite for novelty, which is then killed by boredom as the fashion is duplicated and banalized (as discussed in Chapter 5)? From this perspective, we see fashion built into the modern economy as a sort of obsolescence faster than the wearing out of products, without which many businesses might collapse—were this social function of boredom eliminated. By function, I mean that the motive force of boredom is being used by the social system.

The prevalence is boredom also puts into an interesting light those public personalities called celebrities and stars, idolization of which often approaches that of cult (Klapp, 1969:239–256). Devotees, called fans, follow the career of their hero, mount pictures of him, collect his souvenirs and autographs, wait all night in line to see him in person. Fan magazines and gossip columns supply news of his personal life, no detail of which is too trivial to fascinate the public. If people are vicariously living the careers of celebrities, fulfilling dreams, and possibly getting catharsis from dramas and sports—one might say emotionally hitchhiking on the lives of celebrities—does this not tell us something about boredom with humdrum lives, for which the cult of celebrities is a palliative? In such case, celebrity cult functions not to banish but to compensate for boredom generated possibly elsewhere in the social system.

If so, then it is not at all clear that these three features of modern society—fun industries, fashions, and celebrity cult—banish boredom. One could as plausibly argue that they relieve without remedying it. Analogy with aspirin is appropriate: high usage means not the absence but the presence of pain. Maybe fun industries, fashions, and celebrities are deceptive, and hide boredom under a facade of merriment and diversion which—taken at face value—constitutes false consciousness. So I shall argue in Chapter 10 that fun industries, fads and fashions, and celebrity cult belong in a category with such things as gambling, drug abuse, pinball games, soap operas, Harlequin romances, violent sports and dramas, magic, fortune telling, and astrology, as *placebo* institutions, which produce artificial pleasures and thrills to compensate for lack of such in real life, for, say, the desk-bound and vehicle-confined worker or the housewife puttering among her pots and pans. Such compensations we may take as indicators of boredom, not its absence.

There is no need to overdraw the picture of the prevalence of boredom. By these remarks I undertake no more than to show that boredom is a common experience today—of some people much of the time and almost everyone some of the time. Some people say they have never been bored; but their good fortune hardly negates the fact that others obviously are (and some perhaps unconsciously) enough to constitute a social problem. In this case, analogy with poverty seems appropriate: that some are well fed does not keep others from going hungry. From signs of boredom in work, school, the home, drug abuse, church, politics, sociability; in polls; and depicted in literature; and considering the possible compensatory function of fun industries, fashions, and celebrities, it seems to me that there is a lot of boredom in many sectors of modern life. Surely it is not confined to work but can creep in almost anywhere.

It would be interesting to see a world survey of the prevalence of boredom. I expect that it would show that boredom is a social problem in all modern countries, that advanced technologies and welfare and educational systems—even with the help of fun industries, changing fashions, and celebrities—do not prevent a high level of boredom. It is not surprising that this strange cloud—along with smog—should creep into industrialized societies emphasizing work with machines, uniformity of mass production, consumerism, and satiation from abundance. For the most part of history, boredom was a privilege of the rich; during the eighteenth to twentieth centuries, it became a privilege of common people.

It is an irony of progress that boredom should be high in countries that have the best of it materially, in terms like ease, comfort, convenience, leisure, satiation, low personal output, high expectations, mobility, electronic communication media—all the conditions so familiar to us. Doubtless it was with such irony that Aldous Huxley wrote of a brave new world so afflicted with boredom that it needed antidotes such as Soma and orgies to keep everybody interested. Boredom crept in with progress when least expected. *Hard* work does not cause it; maybe leisure does. Fun industries and fashions do not banish it. Capitalism and socialism both have their share of it. It seems to be a pervasive problem of modern social systems in any part of the world. It is awkward that increasing affluence has not lessened boredom. Whatever progress was for, it was not for that.

Therefore, let us not think of small communities and traditional societies as dull backwaters, from which people need to escape to the excitement and fulfillment of modern city living. These are mere stereotypes. City dwellers often think of rural communities as dull backwaters where nothing much happens. Yet this is contradicted by the intense interest that small towners take in each other and minor happenings, as shown by sociological studies such as Blumenthal (1932) and Christian (1972). Is such interest properly characterized as boredom, or, as I think, a quite different interpretation: warmth of social interest? Proust writes, in *Swann's Way*, of the consternation of his relatives in Combray at the sight of a person they "didn't know at all," requiring instant inquiries as to who the newcomer could be. There was intense interest in the doings of everyone on the street and in all gossip, however seemingly trivial. It is hard to call such interest boredom; and easier to speak so of the indifference of city dwellers toward others, which Georg Simmel called the blasé attitude. Therefore, seeking examples of boredom, let us not think of a farmer leaning on his plough, but of a clerk who stares off into space and yawns while talking to a customer. Do not think of tribal people around a campfire telling their folktales but of modern ones inundated with output of media, switching channels on their television. Do not think only of a man on an assembly line making products he neither knows nor cares about, but also of a man in a reception line greeting people he neither knows nor cares about. Or that man you see on the street, hurrying to meet obligations, talking to people about things that do not interest him, distracted by competing concerns and signals; rushing to lunches, cocktails, dinners; standing in line for entertainments, very active but not involved—busy boredom.

I have tried here to show that boredom is a serious social problem, and that it pervades the social fabric in many sectors beyond work. In literature, especially as ennui, it is a prominent theme signifying lack of meaning in life, with serious consequences.

Regarding its prevalence, I readily concede that evidence is insufficient to show that there is more boredom now than ever, or that there is more or less boredom in various countries, modern and less developed. A baseline is lacking from which one could compare levels of boredom in various places and eras. (Is not the case rather parallel with that of smog, for which there were no readings in Dickens's London) All the same, I think there is reason at least to suspect that boredom is associated with modernity—an affliction of advanced societies and affluent classes. Literature portrays it especially among the well off. Certainly it shows no sign of disappearing with what is called material progress. Nor do pleasures afforded by fun industries, fads, fashions, and the cult of celebrities seem to banish so much as to palliate boredom (see Chapter 10).

However, to see boredom as a social problem, there is no need to prove that it is growing. Plainly it affects a considerable number of people, some transitorily and some deeply, with consequences such as loss of meaning and potential, drug abuse, vandalism, crime, and suicide. Romantics, by their demand for personal fulfillment, deserve credit for helping discover boredom as a systemic problem—not merely a fault of individuals. I think that sociologists will be inclined to agree with romantics that boredom can come from a social system—its structure, institutional dysfunctions, culture, or communication—rather than aberrant individuals.

Another thought worth pursuing is that some boredom is socially constructed in some social classes and groups. The importance of the large vocabulary of English words connoting boredom may be that it not only registers the prevalence of boredom but helps create it. That is, once named, boredom is not just a state of feeling but a concept, a role, a socially constructed reality. The very name might *suggest* being bored; and the role might carry the obligation that one *ought* to be bored in certain company or circumstances. Hence, boredom could become a fashion, or a pose such as that of the blasé aristocrat or of the romantic bohemian.

NOTES

1. *Frequencies of Word Use*

	1931	1961
Boredom	1	11
Monotony	4	7
Routine	15	35
	20	53

Frequencies for 1931 are per million words, from Thorndike and Lorge (1944). For 1961 frequencies are from a corpus of 1,014,232 words, counted by Kucera and Francis (1967).

2. Historian Edmund Goblot (1973:433–44) writes that philistinism was the focus of romantic complaint during the nineteenth and early twentieth centuries.

For the artists and writers of the Romantic era, the "bourgeois" represented the barbarian, the Philistine, the enemy.... Nothing contrasts more with bourgeois life than bohemian living.... In the language of the Romantics the word bourgeois ... denotes the merchant quick to turn a profit, who enjoys ... an abundance of material possessions, who is fond of comfort and who troubles himself little about ideals. "Flaubert had a hatred of the bourgeois," writes his niece.... In his mouth it was synonymous with being mediocre and covetous, living on the pretense of virtue, an insult to all greatness and all beauty.... [The bourgeois man] scorned vain amusements and merely tolerated the ornamental arts, which were really only for the dreamers, the imaginative, the sentimental; for him they could only be relaxation.

3. In Jane Austen's *Sense and Sensibility* (1811), the romantic is sharply portrayed in Marianne Dashwood, who feels that to live impetuously by strong feelings is a virtue, almost a duty; and feels contempt for people who live more safely by conventional and selfish standards. As might be expected, she suffers much by giving her heart to a scoundrel who jilts her. By contrast, her sister, Elinor, stands for sense and self-command—more appreciated in the conventional world of the bourgeois and even of the marriage-arranging nobility.

4. In Herman Hesse's novel *Steppenwolf*, the middle-aged hero, Harry Haller, is a romantic who rages against the boring comfort of German middle-class living; he breaks out by an amorous fling and escapes through the doors of a Magic Theater of drug experimentation.

4

SOCIAL SCIENTISTS' VIEWS

Social scientists have something to say about boredom. While their picture does not disagree in important respects with that from literature in Chapter 2, it does help conceptualize more clearly what boredom is, what conditions give rise to it, what goes on in the process, and (from economists and sociologists) what role boredom might have in a social system.

The usual picture, whether in social science or literature, tends to stress monotony, tedium ("nothing is happening"): restriction or underload of information; whereas the picture that I believe better fits our modern society of high information load is boredom right in the midst of busyness, processing a lot of information that is uninteresting.

The usual picture, I say, stresses *under*load, conceiving boredom as a mental state that arises when one does not get enough interesting information. A person who is getting enough interesting information will not be bored. If his interest is strong, as in a hobby, he can endure, if not enjoy, much information that would bore another. Attention can be attracted and interest aroused by startling or alerting stimuli; but to *sustain* attention, those stimuli must offer something of enough interest. Sheer amount of information—little or much—is not the question. Lack of interest is the heart of boredom.

The restlessness that we take as a sign of boredom (fidgeting, yawning, doodling, sighing) shows that it is, at least in that phase, a *tension*—not mere lassitude, apathy, drowsiness, indifference, or low-frequency EEG waves. In his classic study, psychologist D.E. Berlyne (1960) stressed the active side of boredom, that it is an aversive arousal of a drive which occurs when "external stimuli are excessively scarce or excessively monotonous." Both of these conditions "mean a meager influx of information—in the one case because signals are lacking and in the other case because signals are highly predictable. The drive in question is what we usually call boredom" (p. 187). It "works through a rise in arousal," first expressed in restlessness (actions like doodling) and a tendency to escape physically or by daydreaming or artistic creativity; then it can lead to mounting struggles for variety: "A human being or an animal in the throes of agonizing boredom does not look like a creature with low arousal. On the contrary, he shows the restlessness, agitation, and emotional upset that usually coincide with high arousal" (p. 189).

Boredom leads to exploration of a sort that is *diversive*—seeking "stimulation from any source that is 'interesting' or 'entertaining,' as distinguished from the specific exploration of curiosity." Unlike boredom, the specific exploration of curiosity is interested and arises from different conditions, namely, "uncertainty about a specific environmental object" (Berlyne, 1965:244–245). Qualities such as complexity, novelty, and uncertainty make visual objects interesting, as shown by experimental aesthetic studies (Berlyne, ed., 1974:135, 179). Diversive exploration helps us understand the restless, prying, prowling, prankish side of boredom. It is a form of search, by which humans strive to keep up an optimal level of arousal, tonus, and information intake. Psychological studies describe strategies by which people cope with boredom, such as daydreaming, mental game-playing, motor restlessness, exploration, response variability, and withdrawal from the boring situation (Smith, 1981). So, Kishida (1973) found among 149 female assembly workers subsidiary activities on the job such as chatting, looking around, changing position, arranging hair, and yawning offering some relief from feelings of fatigue, dullness, and shoulder stiffness. However, severe and constant pacing on conveyor lines suppressed such activities even though it increased feelings of fatigue, dullness, and stiffness. This tells us that work pressure can mask boredom by reducing symptoms that normally signify it.

The restlessness of boredom brings up another important aspect, namely, that it occurs when we are forced to give attention to a situation providing too little of what we are interested in—or too much of what we are not interested in. Psychologists find that constraint is a major factor in boredom, including vigilance required for tasks from which attention is not allowed to wander (Smith, 1981). In other words, all boredom is *trapped* in some way, whether it be a classroom, required reading, a concert hall, endless committees, a chore, a long church service, a banquet, a dull party which it is impolite to leave, a conversation which one can neither escape nor get a word in edgewise. (Bore: "A person who talks when you wish him to listen"—Ambrose Bierce.) A person who is able to leave a situation promptly or change an uninteresting subject is unlikely to be bored; at least such a person has the hope of something new and interesting. But one who is stuck in a situation that promises no interesting information, feedback, or meaning will feel bored as soon as the lack of promise becomes evident. It is possible to feel trapped in a culture, an institution, a social class, illustrated by fictional characters such as Herman Hesse's Harry Haller, Sinclair Lewis's Carol Kennicott, Ibsen's Hedda Gabler, or Thomas Mann's Hans Castorp confined in the sanitarium on the magic mountain. Maupassant felt that he was a "prisoner of ennui" all his life, from which his only escape was art. In a letter he wrote: "I am terribly bored.... I accept everything with indifference and I spend two thirds of my time being profoundly bored.... Everything is divisible into farce, ennui, and wretchedness" (Kuhn, 1976:326).

This brings us to a useful distinction between ordinary boredom, often a result of a situation, and *ennui*, a deeper sort, which is not easily attributable to a particular situation, but is chronic, a sense of world-weariness or meaninglessness of life. Kuhn (1976:12–13) distinguishes ennui from more ordinary sorts of boredom by the following characteristics: (1) it involves both body and soul, is spiritual as well as physical; (2) it is independent of external circumstances; (3) it is independent of will; it seizes a person, who becomes "helpless"; (4) it is estrangement, a feeling of meaninglessness or emptiness of the world. An example is Goethe's Faust: on the verge of suicide, relieved from ennui by Satanic assistance; but Mephistopheles "can supply nothing to fill the void in Faust's soul" (pp. 191–193).

Other states, akin to boredom, are often mixed with it. People may not make fine distinctions when they say a situation is dull, tiresome, lacking in zest or that they are "fed up" or "turned off" by it. One such kindred state is drowsiness, a prelude to sleep—and perhaps interesting dreams. But, obviously, drowsiness is not arousing and can occur in many conditions other than boredom, such as fatigue or the effect of a sleeping pill.

Three other states akin to boredom are often part of the picture. All come from repetition or too much of some sensory input. One is *satiation*, loss of appetite signaling having reached a limit of intake, "enough," or "too much," but appetite returns after stimuli become scarce. It presumably plays a larger part in the boredom of affluent than of less developed countries. Satiation interacts circularly with boredom. For example, boredom markedly increases food consumption of both obese and normal people, and obese eat more food when confronted with a boring task (Abramson and Stinson, 1977). Overweight persons, when bored, perceive time to pass more slowly than do normals and eat sooner (Rodin, 1975). Another state often involved with boredom is *habituation*, loss of responsiveness as novelty wears off repeated stimuli (for example, slum dwellers kick cans around until they don't see them; asked by middle-class people what should be done about this mess, they might ask, "What mess?"). A third state akin to boredom is *desensitization*: jading, a loss of sensitivity to increasingly strong stimuli, as when medical professionals become inured to the shock of operations or distasteful chores. Desensitization is systemically used in toughening military recruits and in therapy to overcome troubles such as fear of air travel by exposing patients to a mounting series of anxiety-arousing stimuli. Sometimes boredom is a motive for sensory excesses that lead to jading—a well-known vicious circle.

All of these kindred states—boredom, satiation, habituation, desensitization—may be involved when a job or a life seems monotonous, ho hum, a rut. They have in common lessened stimulation and awareness, a psychological closing. Each has its own contours. The first two fluctuate. But boredom often comes from information *under*load, and is followed by rising restlessness (aversive in tone) and diversive exploration; while satiation comes from stimulus *over*load, and leads to quiescence (normally without aversion) followed by renewed appetite for the same—so the curve fluctuates regularly.

The latter two—habituation and desensitization—lack the fluctuation of boredom and satiation: repeating the same stimulus or progressively stronger stimuli leads to a deadening—a steady decline of arousal, awareness, interest and response amplitude—which may be permanent. One blessing of habituation and desensitization is that they numb us to unavoidable hardships, and give us respite from noise and ugliness that otherwise might produce intolerable stress and boredom.

In modern society our problem is often that we have all four—boredom, satiation, habituation, and desensitization—going at the same time, interacting in unknown ways. The overload of violence in media is a case in point. Does the excitement of violence compensate people for boredom in real life? Does it satiate, hence appease the appetite for violence? Does it habituate people, so that they don't even notice how violent the media are? Does it make people calloused and even bored by violence?

Since these states akin to boredom—satiation, habituation, and desensitization—cause loss of awareness, they may have something to do with the difficulty, mentioned in Chapter 3, of finding out by polls just how many and how often people are bored.

Satiation, habituation, and desensitization result from *over*loads of stimuli. On the other hand, *under*loads of stimuli can cause boredom—the most acute experiences being produced by sensory deprivation, a severe loss of information, produced experimentally by putting people into an environment that is monotonous and artificial, cutting off communication, variety, and activity. The best known early studies (Heron, 1957) stressed its negative effects. For example, men were paid to lie on a comfortable bed around the clock in a lighted cubicle, wearing eye covers admitting diffuse light and gloves and cardboard cuffs to limit touch perception, and meaningful sounds were reduced by soundproofing of the cubicle and a producing masking noise. About the only interesting experiences these men had were eating and trips to the bathroom. Though the pay was good, and there seemed to be hardly any stress, most could stand no more than two or three days. Effects included loss of efficiency in performing tasks, increasing irritability and restlessness, loss of perspective, oscillations in feeling, hallucinations, and slowing brain rhythm. After only four or five hours, they could not follow a connected train of thought and found their ability to concentrate was seriously disturbed for 24 hours or more after coming out of isolation. Woodburn Heron, one of the McGill psychologists, concluded that a changing sensory environment seems essential for normal mental functioning of human beings; variety is not only the spice of life, as the adage says; it is the very stuff of it. Monkeys, too, raised in a box with only a dim light under conditions of sensory deprivation become debilitated or aggressive (Prescott, 1974; Harlow, 1968). Reports from the National Aeronautics and Space Administration (NASA) in 1985 told that space lab and shuttle personnel complained of monotony because the only colors were white and beige, and smells (of coffee, and so on) were absent from the sterile environment. In general, people and animals deprived of sensory input prefer variability, uncertainty, and complexity over redundant patterns of stimuli

(Rapoport and Kantor, 1967). "Normal functioning of the brain depends on a continuing arousal reaction...which in turn depends on constant sensory bombardment" (Heron, 1957:56).

Gradually, however, this picture of need for sensory bombardment changed, as studies of sensory deprivation and stimulus underload mounted until over 3,300 subjects had been covered (Suedfeld, 1975). In this development a shift of emphasis was noted: *Benefits* of underload were being reported, not just adverse effects as in earlier studies. Advantages of the monotonous situation included improved sensory (visual, auditory, tactile) acuity and sensitivity, memorization, and visual concentration; shorter reaction time; and more daydreaming, openness, and creativity. Sensory deprivation also helped therapies such as for stuttering, retarded children's learning ability, contact with autistic children, and stopping smoking. A positive side of monotony had become more apparent: *arousing* subjects to be more aware and ready to change—more open to new experience.

This arousing and opening side takes us to the fact that, although aversive—indeed, because aversive—boredom is not a dead loss but is a useful part of information search when it leads to diversive exploration that can be fun if not educational and creative. Who can say how many works of art and literature are by-products of boredom? Creative responses to boredom are studied by Schubert (1978). Kuhn (1976:378) says that if ennui does not "engulf" its victim, it induces efforts to fill the void; if it does not "render sterile," it makes possible "creation in the realms of the practical, the spiritual and the esthetic." Some swamis, such as Rajneesh (1976:219) hold that the boringness of meditation, for example, japam (mantra repetition), conduces to enlightenment. This role of boredom in information search is further conceptualized in Chapter 8, "A Metaphorical Model."

The main theme we are pursuing here is the relation of information load to boredom—whether a low load (as in sensory deprivation) or a high load is conducive to it, or both, and under what conditions. Some things psychologists tell us may help with this inquiry.

One factor that has much to do with whether a sensory load is experienced as low or high is expectations. If you *expect* a high and interesting load of input, you will be challenged rather than stressed by it and are likely to be dissatisfied and bored by a simple job. So studies have found that easy, simple, undemanding, monotonous jobs are also stressful, contrary to the common assumption that it is high-pressure jobs with long hours that cause stress. Horn (1975) found that a worker with a light load can get "bored to sickness" by stimulus *under*load of monotonous, unchallenging work. For example, the University of Michigan's Research Center for Group Dynamics, comparing occupations, found that doctors, who worked long hours with high responsibility and concentration, were more satisfied with their work and lower in depression, anxiety and irritation than were assembly-line workers, who, with normal work hours and little responsibility, complained most about depression, poor appetite, insomnia, and other physical problems. Along a similar line, a study of 23 occupations (Kaplan, 1975) found that the three most undemanding and boring occupations were assembly-line work, machine tending, and operating a fork lift. Workers on these jobs experienced more psychosomatic complaints and depression than did workers in other jobs, even the most overdemanding ones. Moreover, the higher the education, the more stressful was undemanding work. So expectations rather than sheer load of work can make the genesis of boredom seem to come from underload.

Another study relating boredom to load of information is that of Csikszentmihalyi (1975:35–36, 50), who, studying various professions and hobbies, found that tasks that are too simple are boring, but on the other hand, if they are too complex and demanding, one worries. The ideal state he calls flow, or the "autotelic" experience: zest, involvement, joy in action, whether in work or play. Studying activities such as rock climbing, surgery, and chess, he found that in them performers were able to achieve flow: "complete involvement of the actor with his activity. ... There is no time to get bored or to worry about what may or may not happen..." (pp. 35–36). Flow gives a fulfillment not unlike what Maslow (1962) called peak experience. But flow is in a mid-range between boredom if the task is too simple and worry if it is too demanding and complex. "Flow is experienced when people perceive opportunities for action as being evenly matched by their capabilities. If, however, skills are greater than the opportunities for using them, boredom will follow" (p. 50). Facing the various demands and opportunities of life, we are "poised between boredom and worry."

Other aspects of boredom—chronic rather than situational—are described by psychiatrists who hold that neurotic boredom is due to mechanisms of repression (in our argument a restriction of information), by which a person limits his own life. Bernstein (1975:513, 525–526) says:

The superego has for many grown so restrictive of the experience of intensity of feeling that it creates the chronic boredom that afflicts them.... The superego's repressing barrier spares the individual the uncomfortable experience of anxiety, but . . . it may exert a severe constricting influence upon the individual's capacity to experience intensity . . . then he may be spared the discomfort of anxiety but at the price of chronic boredom.

Likewise, Wangh (1975:538, 545–546) puts the psychoanalytic view this way:

Boredom results from a stalemate between opposing forces in the mind. . . . We discover in the analysis of the complaint of boredom that wish confronts threat. The result is a standoff called boredom. The tension in boredom, then, is an echo of the pressure for action toward some unconscious aim, and the unpleasure an echo of the threat of pain or punishment. A precarious balance is maintained by partial repression of both longed-for content and feared danger. A blasé person must chronically prevent the emergence into consciousness of any fantasy whatsoever. . . . He cannot let us know, any more than he can allow himself to know, what truly might interest and arouse him and thereby make him interesting to us—that is, invite us to participate in his mental life. Inevitably, for this very reason, he also becomes a bore (p. 549).

According to such theory, out of repression can come the deeper sorts of boredom—the sense of hollowness noted in literary portrayals of *tedium vitae*, and even some "blue-collar blues," when they mask deeper symptoms. In such cases, blaming the assembly-line environment may be only a rationalization. A psychiatric field survey of 888 automobile workers engaged in production-line tasks revealed no more evidence of unrelatedness, loneliness, boredom, life dissatisfaction, work dissatisfaction, or depression among them than among their spouses, implying that where such symptoms occur they are *not job situational* but part of a broader pattern of emotional illness (Siassi et al., 1974). Since the psychiatric view weighs early history heavily, it takes in a broader swathe of experience than could be attributed to any job in explaining chronic boredom. For our purposes, neurotic restriction of experience is a sort of *under*load of information, an unconscious albeit voluntary avoidance of facts. A life that is chosen to be a rut is not all that different from a sensory deprivation chamber.

Seemingly opposite to neurotic restriction is the sensation seeker, a personality type who, according to psychologists, is prone to boredom. He needs a higher level of arousal and challenge of variety than do most people. Easily bored in ordinary situations, he seeks sensations that range from making new friends to roaming the world's far-off places, from risky sports to experiments with hallucinogenic drugs, from tasting 37 flavors of ice cream to trying to duplicate the reputed 1,037 seductions of Don Juan. Peter Greenberg (1977) descibes thrill seekers, in sports involving falling, leaping, diving, and so on, who find challenge by taking their lives in their hands. Thrill machines at amusement parks, such as the parachute jump at Coney Island, are continually being improved to meet the public demand to be scared. Another psychologist, Marvin Zuckerman (1978), regards the sensation seeker as a personality type who can be identified on a scale by his preference in answers to questions, such as, "I enter water gradually" versus "I like to dive or jump right in." Such a person seeks adventures in all sensory modalities; and is gregarious, disliking to be alone and quiet; he seeks disinhibition, tension, and arousal, even moderate fear; he needs constant variety in stimuli to reach an optimal level of arousal—hence is easily bored. Indeed, Zuckerman holds that boredom is a motive for sensation seeking, and their need for excitement is why sensation-seekers readily abuse drugs:

When a high sensation-seeker is tied down to a dull, routine kind of job for eight hours a day, he builds up a terrible kind of tension that can lead to the abuse of alcohol or drugs. Some former drug abusers...described how they would have to get drunk or high in order to face a day on the assembly line. Eventually, they came to prefer the risky excitement of drug-related crime to the grinding monotony of their jobs (1978:99).

By the way, studies by J.E. Barnack report that even legal stimulants such as caffeine, ephedrine, and amphetamine reduce boredom (Smith, 1981). And the most consistent finding of psychological research on boredom is that extroverts (more common than sensation seekers) are also especially susceptible to boredom (Smith, 1981), presumably because of their need for much stimulation from other people.

However, we need not take boredom-prone people—extroverts, sensation seekers, or neurotics—as models of typical human behavior. They might lead us to overdraw the picture of boredom in human life, as perhaps did Pascal, who saw man on a sort of treadmill, perpetually needing diversion, and not getting enough, he suffers boredom. Pascal wrote "However happy a man may be, he will soon be discontented and wretched, if he be not diverted and occupied by some passion or pursuit which prevents weariness from overcoming him." And again:

So wretched is man that he would weary even without any cause for weariness from the peculiar state of his disposition; and so frivolous is he, that, though full of a thousand reasons for weariness, the least thing, such as playing billiards or hitting a ball, is sufficient to amuse him (*Pensees*, Number 139).

It seems doubtful that most people are such unwearying sensation seekers. Perhaps Pascal was describing neurotic ennui. He might have stressed the opposite picture—as do Buddhists—that people who unwearyingly seek sensations are the more bored, that one can get bored by *too much* variety, as we shall suggest in Chapters 7 and 9.

Since sensation seekers shun boredom actively, it is interesting to note their possible linkage with romanticism, already mentioned as having helped discover boredom as a social problem. Presumably, sensation seekers, feeling hunger for variety sooner and more keenly than the average, swell the ranks of bored romantics (was Byron a sensation seeker?), and so by their restlessness—in adventures, protests, rebellions, and the like—serve as important indicators of the scope of the problem. If sensation seekers are compensating by thrills for a meaning deficit in the social system, then thrill seeking, hedonism, and sensuality could mean just the opposite of what they seem to—not proof of how exciting and fulfilling life is but of how tedious and empty—especially when jading takes its toll from pleasures.

To sum up, sensation-seekers and extroverts exhibit a picture of people hungry for input, gregarious, needing arousal, seeking adventure, therefore having a low threshold of boredom. What might be normal existence for others is monotony to them. Again, expectations are a problem. They feel restricted, that is, percieved *under*load is the cause of their boredom. In this respect, life perceived as a rut is not all that different from a sensory deprivation chamber.

So far we have treated boredom as an individual experience; but there is the obvious question: What is it about a social structure or communication system or culture that causes boredom? Economists and sociologists have had something to say about this.

Economists have most often found systemic sources of boredom in two main places: production, where boredom affects motivation to work; and consumption, where deprivation and satiation are both key concepts.

On the score of conditions of work, the theory of alienated labor, stemming from Marx, holds that mechanization and specialization of labor which developed under industrial capitalism forced people into a dehumanized existence, in which the product of their labor had no real meaning to them; workers became estranged from their work and from themselves. From an economic point of view, boredom expressing alienation from work means loss of productivity and a personnel morale problem, even when more than compensated by labor-saving machines.

The other systemic source of boredom to which economists have paid most attention is the impact of production upon consumers in the mass market, namely, satiation by commodities. Scitovski (1976) attributed much of the "joylessness" of the modern economy to boredom from passive consumption requiring little effort and skill and so not enriching life culturally or developing abilities in consumers. He showed by time-budget analysis how American consumers, with the help of producers, have opted for comfort rather than active skill in living.

Hirschman (1982) also theorized about the impact of production upon consumers. He saw an interesting cycle in which boredom generates oscillation between private interest and public action. Consumers are bored by durable goods they avidly seek but in which they lose interest once possessed. Disappointed by pursuing private interests, they turn to public actions in the political sphere. That, in turn, disappoints, since political expectations are even harder to fulfill than economic ones. People turn again to the private sector for gratification. So the cycle of frustration and boredom goes on.

Regarding our theme of underload and overload, alienated labor seems to be a deprivation of meaning, whereas Scitovsky and Hirschman emphasize satiation as a factor in consumption, market behavior, and even politics.

Among sociologists, Max Weber is outstanding in having developed a theory of social organization that implies boredom in almost every joint, especially of bureaucracy, that form of rational order in which officials follow minutely detailed rules without discretion, reducing work to simple routines (performable by anyone) that bore officials quite as much as they do clients wearied by red tape. So Weber conceived of bureaucracy as restricting the individual, antagonistic to charisma, almost by definition boring. His broader conception was of rationalization as a historical process which, while it built order, did so by routines taking the place of tradition and charisma, and by scientific matter-of-factness disenchanting the world—again strongly implying boredom in the form of existential ennui.

On the score of underload/overload, Weber saw rational social organization as a system which, however efficient, denied personnel meaning and information for larger decisions, and disenchanted (alienated) them—deprivations.

Another outstanding sociologist, Charles H. Cooley (1927), had bureaucracy in mind when he developed his broader concept of *formalism* as a fault of social structure, when social activity deteriorates into sterile, mechanical procedure, and

social relations fall to a low plane—just as a teacher who has too much to do necessarily adopts a mechanical style of instruction. So what we call "red tape" prevails in great clerical offices (p. 56).... A merely formal politeness goes with a crystallized society, indicating a certain distrust of human nature and desire to cloak or supplant it by propriety (p. 198).... Too much mechanism in society gives us something for which there are many names ... institutionalism, formalism, traditionalism, conventionalism, ritualism, bureaucracy, and the like.... Mechanism ... becomes an evil ... when it interferes with growth and adaptation ... suppresses individuality and stupefies or misdirects the energies of human nature (p. 342) ... so long as spirit and symbol are vitally united and the idea is really conveyed, all is well, but so fast as they are separated the symbol becomes an empty shell, to which, however, custom, pride or interest may still cling. It then supplants rather than conveys the reality. Underlying all formalism, indeed, is the fact that it is psychically cheap; it substitutes the outer for the inner as more tangible, more capable of thought and feeling, more easily extended, therefore, and impressed upon the multitude. Thus in ... architecture or literature we have innumerable cheap, unfelt repetitions of forms that were significant and beautiful in their time and place. The effect of formalism upon personality is to starve its higher life and leave it the prey of apathy, self-complacency, sensuality (p. 343). ... The apparent opposite of formalism, but in reality closely akin to it, is disorganization or disintegration ... one is mechanism supreme, the other mechanism going to pieces (p. 347).

Cooley's concept is broader than Weber's because formalism can develop outside bureaucracy, in any social structure—even, one might suppose, friendship or parent-child relations. It consists of substituting a shell—some role, procedure, mechanism, or symbol—which denies spontaneous, sincere interaction, separates people, and produces apathy.

Clearly Cooley's is a deprivation view. He describes a cold, impersonal structure, in which people lack warm feelings and relations are hypocritical (a shell), so personality is "starved"—a denial or restriction, which might be investigated as an underload of stimuli and information.

Another concept of boring social structure developed by sociologists

is that of ritualism, the vain performance of actions known to be inef-
fectual or which have lost their purpose. Sociologists define it as: "displacement of goals whereby an instrumental value becomes a terminal
value" (Merton, 1949:154–155); or members of an organization becoming "so preoccupied with meticulous application of detailed rules that
they lost sight of the very purpose of their action" (Blau, 1956:87–88).
Ritualism is not healthy ritual (the heart of communal and traditional
societies—and of religion itself, according to Durkheim) but a form of
anomie, a sterile, hollow procedure, in its perfunctoriness and lack of
value-product almost necessarily boring. Ritualism might be found in
bureaucracy, but is not the same as bureaucracy, and can occur outside
it. It may be only another aspect of the formalism described by Cooley.
On the score of underload/overload, ritualism is plainly a deprivation of
meaning and purpose in repeated actions.

Concerning ritualism as a form of anomie takes us back to Emile
Durkheim, who theorized in a way that helps explain boredom produced
by *variety*, rather than monotony—important for the view we shall offer,
that boredom results as often from too much information as too little.
Durkheim held that anomie, loss of social regulation, exposes people to
a range of choices ungoverned by rules of fixed status, a pursuit of
novelties that is not only demoralizing but frustrating and boring. As
Durkheim explained: disintegration of social bonds, especially rapid rises
of status, remove needed constraints from the individual, opening him
to boundless desires and insatiable striving which result not in happiness
but boredom. Anomie gives rise to "greed," also a thirst "for novelties,
unfamiliar pleasures, nameless sensations, all of which lose their savor
once known." The pursuit of such pleasures is endless and futile.

Pleasure ... loses its intensity through repetition.... To the extent that we ac-
custom ourselves to a certain type of happiness, it flees from us, and we are
obliged to throw ourselves into new undertakings to recapture it. We must
bring the extinguished pleasure to life again by means of more energetic stimuli
(1947:252).

In this view, Durkheim did not distinguish boredom from its kindred
state, jading (desensitization), as we have previously done. But he did
distinguish useless novelty, by which we are jaded, from the variety
necessary to happiness (1947:253). Anomic pursuit of novelties helps us
to see what I would call the less recognized side of boredom: that variety,

not just monotony and restriction of sensory input, can produce it. We shall argue that too much variety as well as too little can be meaningless and boring.

Durkheim's is a satiation view of the causes of boredom. Lack of regulation (restriction) leads to excessive freedom, an unrestricted pursuit of sensations, which leads to boredom as satiation. This is an overload view.

Another theory of how boredom arises from social structure is that of Zijderveld (1979), who notes that our lives are mediated more by clichés than by deeply felt and understood symbols. These clichés are a product of the very rationality (in Max Weber's and Ferdinand Toennies's sense) of social structure, the necessity for dealing expeditiously with strangers with whom we share no ground of claims or history for loyalty or communal meaning. Clichés are "mental moulds," expressions whose "semantic vigor" has been worn out by "repetitive use." They work like coins in a slot, to "trigger" behavior and enable us to interact "routinely" and "mechanically" without empathy or role-taking (pp. 13–14, 58). Modernity generates clichés by its demand for functional rationality (emphasizing means above ends and functions above meanings), saying, in effect, "Get on with it, never mind what you feel." We no longer can rely on deeper traditional meaning: modernization (industrialization, urbanization, rise of science and technology, bureaucratization, and the capitalist mode of production) has wiped it out and brought about the "supersedure of meaning by function" (p. 46). So clichés fill a void. But they are felt as objective, repressive, abstract, and alienating (pp. 37–40). And they are boring—such boredom being, one might say, the price we pay for dealing with large numbers of people in a formal, impersonal way. Clichés are inherently boring because their meaning has been lost. Not only that, but they distort the sense of time. Modern time awareness is absorbed by clock time, while meaningful subjective time (based on institutions, communal and kinship bonds, ritual calendar, and so on) "dwindles and atrophies" (pp. 75–76). Busy people fill up clock-time with countless actions that are functionally rational but not meaningful in terms of subjective time. So they experience boredom in spite of being busy, resulting from the fact that "subjective time is experienced ... as endlessly long" while in clock time "life rushes by" (p. 77). So, by its functional rationality encapsulating people in clichés, modern societies are in danger of erecting the "iron cage" of which Weber wrote (p. 17).

To sum up, Zijderveld theorizes (as did Weber) that boredom comes from the very rationality of social organization. It arises like Weber's routine, from the rational desire to gain efficiency in interaction. But the loss is in subjective meaning. This seems to be an *under*load view: boredom comes from restriction of information needed for meaning.

These views of economists and sociologists give us at least one thing: a recognition that boredom can systematically arise from social structure or the lack of it. It is a problem of a social system, not just of individuals who happen to perceive life in a certain way. If boredom is a problem of society or culture, then millions can be affected in the same way. What is more, we look for something shared—such as communication— to explain shared experience. I do not presume to try to sum up here all the views and findings of social scientists about boredom. We shall take up one thread, that modern social systems generate and modern culture is full of *overloads* of certain kinds of information, to be described in following chapters. The main point here is that psychologists, psychiatrists, economists, and sociologists have recognized what fiction also shows, that there are two sides to boredom: underload and overload.

Most of the views and studies reviewed have stressed *under*loads: monotony, restriction, sensory deprivation, isolation, repression, insufficient complexity, disappointment of expectations, or lack of meaning, as causes of boredom. That is all to the good, but is it the way to describe the stimulus-loaded world of today? Tomblike isolation and sensory deprivation seem too drastic to tell much about the monotony, say, of a clerk in a department store or a bureaucrat pushing paper. Still less do they apply to the sensory *over*loaded part of modern life, where people are busy—highly engaged, distracted by trivia—yet bored. Except for monastics, most of us are inundated with stimuli and information. Affluent societies plainly favor overloads of commodities and communication, and hence boredom from satiation, habituation, and desensitization.

There are, then, two sides to boredom. We contrast situations in which life can be characterized as *underloaded* (lonely, isolated, uneventful, monotonous, stagnant, restricted, simple, tedious, deprived) and *overloaded* (crowded, busy, changing, exposed, bombarded, distracted, complicated, hurried, hectic, satiated). We note that boredom is not confined to the first group but amply distributed in both groups. So we need to enlarge the common picture of boredom as monotony, dullness, "nothing happening," to include the other picture of much happening, a high intake of stimuli, yet boredom—busy boredom, which arises when pace gets faster, change lacks meaning, and movement lacks arrival.

Generally speaking, I would say that social science, though recognizing both, has emphasized underload and neglected overload as a source of boredom. Although there are situations of extreme restriction, monotony, isolation, sensory deprivation, and so on, by and large overload is more important as a cause of boredom than is underload in an information society. Historically, the picture I see is movement away from underload toward overload. Just as, economically, developing societies shift from poverty to plenty, from starvation to satiation, so with information, they shift from scarcity to overload as modern media systems generate more information than people can assign meaning to. A general shift seems to be happening from scarcity toward overload in modern life.

Henceforth, this book will be concerned with why and in what ways modern society produces information overloads that generate boredom. To visualize the alternatives more clearly, let us take three hypothetical cases of boredom. The situation is a compartment of a train on a long trip, which has few views of scenery or other interest from the window, and there are no reading materials, games, cassettes, or other sources of amusement. A passenger is already in the compartment. Another boards. Let us visualize three kinds of traveling companion the newcomer might prove to be. (1) Suppose he is taciturn. For the whole trip, this might be said to be an *under*load of information likely to contribute to boredom, especially in the absence of diversions. (2) Suppose he talks too much about a few subjects, that is, repeats a few views, colloquialisms, stories, and so on monotonously and endlessly. This could be called an *overload* of *redundant* information, no less likely to produce boredom than would be silence. (3) Suppose he is garrulously talkative, and rambles on about everything without discrimination as to relevance, triviality, and so on. Such a companion would be at least as boring as the silent one. Let us call this *overload* of *variety* (of information).

If we drop from consideration underload of communication, illustrated by case number one, there remain two sorts of overload: case number 2, too much redundancy, or information experienced as boring sameness; and case number 3, too much variety of information experienced as irrelevant, trivial, meaningless, and so on, that is, noise.

In broader perspective, what we are dealing with is an imbalance, a distortion of communication, in which personal input mostly from media is too high and output too low in modern life. The media system has helped bring about this imbalance in which people listen more than they talk and sing: the load from the media is so heavy that it is stifling human expression; while overwhelming our ears it denies us a voice. Boredom is a symptom of such a condition, and also a tactic—one of the means by which we fend off excessive information.

Let us now look at overload of redundancy in modern culture.

5

CREEPING BANALITY

"An irremediable flatness is coming over the world"
—William James (1899:59)

A sense of sameness grows in the world in spite of increasing information, speed and range of travel, complexity of organization, reach of communication, pace of fashion, and hours of entertainment. In this chapter we consider one of two major sorts of overload that lead to boredom: redundancy.

Some artists point at banality but do not speak. Klaes Oldenburg's sculpture of a giant hamburger, exhibited at the Ontario Museum of Art in Toronto, is over seven feet in diameter and is made of brown painted sail cloth stuffed with foam rubber, with a green pickle slice on top.

Cartoonist Saul Steinberg was perhaps pointing to the same thing when he found a threat in fluff. Often he draws a conflict between a hero and a dragon. In one such drawing the monster has become an enormous furry rabbit. Steinberg points out:

The rabbit is as armored as the dragon. It has the impenetrable armor of fat fluff. It is invincibly sweet. There are, you see, two sorts of danger. One is being hit by a giant boulder: the direct assault of the world. The other is being overcome by a mountain of fluff, or molasses. The softness is as dreadful as the hardness (Hughes 1978:64).

It may be hard to convince a person excited by the glitter of goods in a department store, or flashing of neon signs, or the marquees of new shows, or spangles of theatrical costumes, that he is getting merely a gawdy surface, a fluff without substance.

We see cultural banality almost everywhere, in ticky-tacky subdivisions, bureaucratic cubicles, assembly lines, concrete jungles, public parking structures, endless miles of highway, billboards, a choice of a Howard Johnson's in 10 miles or a Howard Johnson's in 30 miles.

What is banality? A dictionary defines banal as "lacking freshness and vigor because commonplace or hackneyed; trite; flat; as a banal remark.— Syn. See insipid" (*Webster's New Collegiate Dictionary*, Springfield, Mass.: G. & C. Merriam Co., 1961). Words like commonplace, hackneyed, and trite imply too much redundancy. Insipidity (blandness, sterility, lack of spice) also can be understood as lack of information. We may think of banality as that sort of experience or part of culture which tells nothing new, and the more it is repeated the less it says. Saying nothing new, it is like noise in its lack of message, and also because its repetition is at expense of other, valuable information one might have received. Banality is commonly experienced as monotony "sameness or want of variety, especially wearisome sameness." Jean Renoir (1974) said, "I have no hesitation in attributing the wave of boredom sweeping over the modern world to the monotony of the background against which we live."

Saying so little, banality is an inert ingredient in communication, like paraffin in gasoline. Inattention is an almost automatic response. Unnoticed, it creeps steadily and quietly into modern life. Finally, we can be surrounded by banality, yet unaware of it.

But banality isn't all soft and quiet. There is a noisy sort called kitsch, which fairly screams for attention. It is egregious rather than insipid. One thinks of knicknacks like Eiffel Tower ashtrays, black jockey lawn figurines, souvenirs cheaply reproduced. As one sees it in collections (Dorfles, 1969; Sternberg, 1971; Brown, 1975; Schrank, 1977), it is garish, gawdy, blatantly fake, or falsely sentimental, art that catches the eye and amplifies the worst. Executing in large scale and loud colors what otherwise might not be noticed, it makes the gimcrack gigantic. With the help of mass merchandising and the media, it does not merely creep but explodes in tidal waves of kitsch like that which flowed over the country when Elvis Presley died—200 million records, almost 10 million copies of more than a dozen books, souvenirs ranging from Elvis Presley bubblegum to $50 china busts, Elvis lookalikes crowding the entertainment field (Graham, 1978).

Banalization is an information loss that comes from trying to say more by mere repetition or enlargement, and while saying nothing new, leaving out variety and authentic information, filtering gritty reality into an experience that seems bland, sterile, shallow or insipid. The simplest way to banalize something is to multiply it endlessly. Warhol banalized Marilyn Monroe—already a mass-produced ikon of popular culture—by repeating her image in a sort of wallpaper design. Suppose one repeated the Mona Lisa in a wallpaper design, or exhibited the same landscape by Constable in every living room—such treatment could soon turn even fine art into cliché.

Of course, in our technological society, a chief source of banality is substituting *mechanical* for *organic* form. The hand-worked sculpture, the slightly imperfect pot, the rug whose pattern is in the mind of the weaver, is replaced by a precisely made one instantly recognizable as machine-made. Straight lines and geometrical forms, so rare in nature, in great numbers give a sense of sterile uniformity even when coming in various combinations, sizes,and shapes; that is, to vary a straight line by a right angle or perfect circle is hardly a relief from mechanical form. Substituting mechanical for organic form is basically the reason John Ruskin deplored precision in art. He held it is dead; it makes cheap and easy "that whose difficulty is its honour"; all it does is "make us shallower in our understanding, colder in our hearts, and feebler in our wits." Gombrich (1979:39, 129), quoting Ruskin, concurs. The deadness of mechanical form is due to a "surfeit of redundancies"; if we get "no fresh jolts" to our mind, the "effect is monotony." A similar criticism is made of architectural structures imposed without regard for time and setting, by Robert L. Geddes, Dean of Princeton University's School of Architecture and Urban Planning, who says: "Unless buildings ... really relate to actual human purpose, you end up with little more than an expression of engineering techniques.... Form [is] ... not something that is formulated, *a priori* and foisted upon a situation" (Marlin, 1977). Decisions to foist mechanical form onto naturally varying settings—the thrust of the bulldozer, the concrete sidewalk in place of the footpath— occur so automatically in the modern mind that they seem like a law of growth, which Jacques Ellul (1965:79–111) called "technical automatism," based on a presumption coming from technology itself that there is "one best way" which justifies displacing all others—against which a growing number of people protest, "Small is beautiful" (Schumacher, 1973). The point is that mechanical form, even when handsome and efficient, is more often banal than is organic form.

Let us look at some more sources of banality, beginning with the largest scale, a protest by ecologists that the environment is being destroyed and the world is losing biological variety for the sake of a global monoculture. Few need to be reminded that the world's biological variety is declining. (One ecologist [Myers, 1979] reports that the world is losing a species a day.) But on the cultural side it is as with species: variety is decreasing. Indigenous cultures have been disappearing faster than anthropologists can study them. Modernization destroys traditional ways of living and for large kinship units substitutes bureaucracy and the nuclear family with its almost monotonously familiar tensions and problems.

One sign of loss of the world's indigenous cultural variety is vanishing languages and dialects. Some languages, such as Breton, are dying; others are dead, such as Manx, Asak (Africa), or Algonquin, of which the last native speaker died. In New Guinea alone, there are some 700 different languages, all presumably in danger of being lost. In the United States, dialects are declining under the impact of radio and television. "Soon we'll talk alike," says linguist Martha C. Howard, who has made a study of West Virginia dialects for the *Linguistic Atlas of the United States and Canada* (*The Futurist*, April 1979, p. 80).

Native peoples abandon not only their languages but entire traditions for modernization. Some, such as the Hopi, Basques, and Welsh, fight delaying actions to preserve the languages and faiths of their forebears; but most give up their ways easily. For example, an authority on the Bedouins of Arabia, Wilfred Thesiger, laments their quitting nomadic life. Upon returning to visit them: "All my old friends had moved into concrete houses.... Whenever they move, they hop into a Land Rover. ... Their sons will never know ... desert life.... It's all finished. It just isn't there any more.... It is now tourist buses and transistor radios and airplanes and Land Rovers" (Cowley, 1980). Likewise, the Lapps of Sweden, exposed to television, radio, cars, snowmobiles, and aircraft, are quitting their reindeer-following way of life (few keep herds) and settling down. So also, Eskimos seem content to give up hunting, go on welfare, and chip away at kitsch replicas of their former art for the tourist market.

Modern people, feeling secure in technology, may be content to see the world forget how to use a sacred herb, weave a waterproof basket, or sew an Eskimo boot; but does it not seem ethnocentric to assume that all Western ways, say of child rearing, are superior to those being lost? Margaret Mead has been eloquent in pointing out the loss:

The people ... are losing their old cultures, forgetting how to dance, abandoning the costumes that fitted so spectacularly with the way they moved and spoke.

Once lost, these cultures will be gone irretrievably, lost to their descendents, and lost to the world. . . . If we saw someone standing beside a deep lake, letting priceless, finely wrought ancient Cretan and Egyptian and Incan ornaments slip one by one into the water, there would be an outcry. But . . . ways of life developed through thousands of years are being let go with hardly a murmur from the surrounding world (Loercher, 1977).

Aware of such loss, anthropologists are trying to salvage what they can of the world's perishing cultural store; laboriously reconstructing the Natchez Indian language from tape recordings of the last native speaker; an Algonquin Indian managed to write a phonetic dictionary of his tongue before his people forgot how to pronounce it; institutions like the Smithsonian, the American Museum of Natural History, the Ethnographic Film Commission under UNESCO, and the Folklore Section of the Library of Congress are filming and recording legends, speech, music, dance, customs, crafts, dress styles, and so on before it is too late. The chief of the National Anthropological Film Center, Dr. E. Richard Sorenson, sees his mission as trying to outrun the "cultural convergence" that is homogenizing the societies of the world. Over the millennia humankind have developed rich and varied ways of meeting the problem of living, but these ways are going fast: "We are on the verge of losing that knowledge for all time. Within ten more years it will be gone" (New York Times Service, October 29, 1975). Some (Bodley, 1974) write of modernization as cultural ethnocide. Sociologist Elihu Katz (1977) holds that one of the biggest costs of modernization is destruction of ethnic identity, a sense of who one is as belonging to a people. Folk arts die, often to be replaced by popular culture diffused by media. So musicologist Alan Lomax (1977) laments the fact that the fascinating variety of authentic folk music one might have heard going from village to village in Europe is being replaced by uniform pop, from an "over-centralized electronic communication system" that is "imposing a few standardized, mass-produced and cheapened cultures everywhere."

Thus, popular culture plays an enormous part in making the world's people more alike, because, whatever the political, economic, and ideological differences, Russians may want the same sorts of pop culture as Americans, or South Africans, or Brazilians. From China come reports of youth preoccupied with novelties such as TV sets, permanent waves, smooching in public parks, dark glasses from Hong Kong, and Western movies (Critchfield, 1980). Popular culture consists of cultural forms that have the widest and quickest circulation (including fads, fashions, popular songs and singers, commercial art, jokes, cartoons, clichés, stereotypes, vogue words, fizzy beverages, hit films and TV programs, television commercials, advertising slogans, idols of media and sport, games, gambling, tavern drinking, and other leisure activities). Most of it comes not from indigenous and local roots but from exogenous sources, such as urban manufacture, international trade, mass media, rumor, and imitation of celebrities. So popular culture spreading over society is a veneer which displaces but does not replace indigenous culture, because it is "imposed from above," fabricated by technicians hired by businessmen (Macdonald, 1957:60), and does not send down deep roots; people "grow up with" it, but parents do not share the same pop culture with children, and much of it is soon passé for all. Yet, shallow though it is, it is able to smother indigenous culture, replacing folk tales by TV comics, or crafts by kitsch (Schrank, 1977:18); or smoothing authentic into commercial versions (such as "old time" country music on amplified guitars, in which Appalachia, West Virginia, and Georgia are indistinguishable). Though quickly shared, popular culture does not knit people together as did a folk dance, but, like a discotheque is used by audiences who do not relate to one another beyond the moment.

A strong impetus to the spread of popular culture comes from celebrity models such as movie, TV, and sports idols, whose "hits" propel them to fortune and fame and whose life-styles are imitated not only at home but worldwide. Such imitation adds to the prevalence and redundancy of popular culture. So it is not surprising that, seeing blue jeans and Pepsi and hearing the same popular songs in widely different countries, one realizes that the world's popular culture is becoming a soup with the same noodles floating in it.

Seeing the world's loss of variety, it is hardly surprising that travelers should complain of growing sameness of places—a sterility summed up in Gertrude Stein's remark, "There's no there there." A Canadian voyager, arriving at the Arctic port of Inuvik after a 2,000-mile canoe trip, reported: "They had A and W drive-ins, take-out pizza and chain store hardwares...I couldn't believe it. It was just like being home in Grand Bend" (Wainman, 1978). A man from Omaha visiting the Sahara expects to see a tribal Arab on a camel, just as that same Arab visiting Omaha would like to see a real Sioux Indian brave in headdress. Neither is likely to get what he wants. Western dress is spreading, and display of native costumes is declining all over the world (unless on market or feast days).

And often it is only a show for tourists, who see natives obligingly posing in costumes to give them what they expect and perhaps will pay money to photograph. The more tourists come, the more standardized, staged, and inauthentic the arrangements become (MacCannell, 1973, 1976). Bullfighting, for example, has become a parody of its former self, the bulls weakened and toreros performing showy stunts that disgust real aficionados. So travel becomes ever more banal, as tourists find Kentucky Fried Chicken in Barbados, McDonald's hamburgers in Tokyo, Holiday Inns in the Holy Land, a gigantic Coca Cola bottle alongside the gold pagodas of Bangkok, while authentic exotic experience retreats before them like a will-o'-the-wisp. Of course, the very horde of tourists physically helps to make travel more similar everywhere. "The constant wear and tear from hundreds and thousands of feet and hands," as the custodian of Canterbury Cathedral put it, require that famous places such as Stonehenge or the Altamira Caves of Spain be roped off to spare them further attrition (Jenson, 1979). So tourism becomes more and more an experience of traveling in platoons, finding locked doors, queuing, following guides, and tipping various importunate strangers. Thus tourism (with the best intentions of supplying authentic experience) plays its part in banalization. The ultimate banality of travel is offered by Disney Enterprises' World Showcase, in which one does not go anywhere at all but visits imitation places, such as a Costa Rican fishing village, Japanese feudal fortress, or Moroccan walled city.

Because it has an important part in cultural homogenization, fashion change is worth a closer look, helping us see how redundancy exhausts itself as information. Racks of discarded clothing, blue jeans for $60, former best-sellers (in paperback) for 10 cents, music hits with a life span of months, tell of the importance of fashion change in urban life and world culture. Much of the expense of modern living is keeping pace with fashion. Some say fashion costs too much. But others argue (perhaps after viewing the sartorial drabness of mainland China) that the change and extravagance of fashion add zest to living. I would say that the novelty of fashion does seem to promise a remedy for boredom; but that it is a false hope, for soon one notices that all fashions are imitated. Mass merchandising, cheaply reproducing the latest fashions within weeks, floods the world with copies of copies, enabling everyone to enter the fashion race. Quickly copied, the new fashion drowns in its own redundancy, becoming as banal as what it replaced.

The cycle of adoption and discard follows the familiar S-curve. Going up this slope is like a ride in a ski lift, but coming down is like a fall off a cliff. Rise and decline are especially sudden in the case of fads. The reason for this devaluation is neither loss of utility nor mere satiation (being "tired of," "fed up with" a commodity) but is a loss of signaling function.

We see better what fashion is about if we look on it as a process of self-dramatization, in which "props" such as garments, beverages, automobiles, and so on are used to produce "looks" and images (impressions). Fashionable people shop for "looks" by which to enhance their status. The city is aptly described as a bazaar of people, in which we shop not only for economic goods and wages but experiences, entertainments, styles, status symbols, even ideas and faiths. Media are showcases of fashion. People scan the media for looks and models. (A typical women's magazine might offer a choice of looks, labeled as ethnic, Victorian, Egyptian, Mandarin, coolie, Sailor, Crusader, Alpine, Bedouin, Russian, Musketeer, gypsy, Edwardian, ruffles-and-lace, and so on.) Achieving a look may go beyond dress, cosmetics, and hairstyles to grooming (Wax, 1957), even name-changing, face lifting, and surgical operations. Men often achieve looks by vehicles and sports equipment. Youth may try to achieve a look by slang, a haircut, or manner of manipulating a cigarette or beverage.

In any case, the purpose of looks is to dramatize oneself and convey an impression to others that will earn credit (prestige, glamor, or whatever): perhaps a claim to belong to a certain social set, or an impression to improve—or at least preserve—one's social rating in the eyes of others. If everyone's rating were known and fixed, as in a military rank system, there would be little place for fashion. But the very anonymity and heterogeneity of people in the urban setting make fashion signals almost necessary to tell where people fit. And the high expectations of urban life (stimulated by advertising) favor fashion, because almost everyone is, so to speak, on the make—in some position on a ladder he or she is trying to climb. In an open society, all can gain, and even the wealthiest bolster their standing, by making a good impression: looking one's best, driving a new car, living at a fashionable address, trimming one's lawn, seeing the latest show, and so on. For most people, fashion is a major way, by looks alone, to give oneself a promotion, so to speak. One who takes up a startling or "high" fashion can have an adventure in identity like wearing a costume in a play (Klapp, 1969:75–95). The style displayed may be the only basis by which to rate a person (no matter that his automobile is rented, yacht is borrowed, posh address temporary, "old school tie" not his own—even that his letterhead or certificate is fake). It serves, just as a seemingly large roll of bills does, to impress at the moment people who probably will not have opportunity or time to check further on the validity of the token. The fashion user astutely seeks tokens that will give the maximum credit in impression and rating in return for the cost in effort and money.

But, alas, the message of the fashion is not stable; it may not continue to confer prestige, glamor or elite status. On the contrary, it may signal that the displayer is "out of it," lacking in smartness or distinction. The instability comes from the relative number and position of others imitating the fashion. Soon "everyone" seems to have taken it up; and the elite who started it have moved on to new styles. The increase in supply of the fashion comes from imitation and a sort of Gresham's law in which cheaper copies and even counterfeits flood the market. What it comes to is that the signal doesn't work very well when too many people are making it. A signal can fail because it is redundant, that is, gives no interesting news, tells again what everybody knows—worse, repeats pseudo-information (as in the "Wolf, wolf" fable). So a fashion "look" repeated too often is no longer useful for signaling taste and distinction but loses ability to set the sender apart or identify him with elite status and knowledge (the elite already having moved on to new styles and knowledge), as explained long ago by sociologist Georg Simmel (1957:543–547). The same point could be made by the example of an army giving out too many medals. "When everybody can be anybody, then nobody can be somebody," wrote Gilbert and Sullivan.

So I argue that boredom heralds the end of a fashion when redundancy impairs its function as a signal to gain prestige or even be interesting. So in the early phase of fashion the appetizer of novelty and distinction proves to be a cheat, for, when the main course comes on, it turns out to be a dull dish of conformity rather than adventure of identity and taste.

It seems unavoidable that media are banalizing, because they say the same thing to more and more people more often; are inherently duplicative, repetitive, and diffusive; and even the freest of media tailor their messages to the "mass mind."

There is no need to suppose that centralized control and propaganda are necessary to make them so. A number of studies show that free enterprise in broadcasting, recording, and publishing in America is no guarantee of diversity of output, and that the corporate and commercial organization of the media contributes to uniformity. An entire issue of the *Journal of Communication* (Volume 28, Spring 1978) was devoted to exploring why the United States, with three competing television networks and over 8,000 stations, of which hundreds are independent, had not gained more diversity in programming, declining diversity from 1953 to 1974 being shown by a chart (Dominick and Pearce, 1976). According to studies of television in both Canada and America (Nelson, 1979:18):

fewer and fewer types of programs are taking up increasing amounts of broadcast time. Currently, the two staples of commercial prime time are the sitcom and the crime series. Much as soap operas and game shows have tended to dominate daytime hours, these two formulas are the backbone of prime time.... Basically, the sponsor always plays it safe: avoiding controversy, opting for the familiar, relying on the tried-and-tested formulas.

In America three television networks—ABC, NBC, and CBS—dominate because they "have 95 percent of the nation hooked into their outlets"—a control so strong that some corporations, such as Mobil, are demanding a fourth network (Hurwitz, 1978:74). Such ownership stifles local programming (Litman, 1978:51) and monopolizes the audience (Jacklin, 1978:88). Westen (1978) explains why conformity is inherent in the United States system of television broadcasting, illustrating by cases of corporate editing. So far cable television has not lived up to its promise of diversity, being in danger of control by one or two networks (Brunner and Chen, 1978:81–84).

Likewise, for the popular music industry in America, a study (Rothenbuhler and Dimmick, 1982) showing that from 1974 to 1980 it became more concentrated, the number of competing firms declining, while products lost diversity. The number of firms with hits fell by over half, from 21 in 1975 to 9 in 1980. The top four firms had most of the hits, their share gaining from 51 percent in 1976 to 76 percent in 1980. Concentration of hit recordings among a few successful producers has increased. The authors explain why diversity is lost: "Any one producer can only be capable of a few styles and most successful producers have a single distinctive style for which they are known.... This increasing reliance on a few producers can be expected to produce only homogeneity in the musical product" (p. 147).

In the publishing industry also there were signs of concentration and threat of decreasing diversity. During the 1970s it was noted with concern that business conglomerates (such as Litton Industries, the Xerox Corporation, and ITT) were taking over publishing houses. Not only that, but publishing houses such as Harper and Row and Lippincott were merging and buying paperback houses; more than 300 such corporate mergers and acquisitions having occurred in recent years. Most concern was caused by *communication* conglomerates, such as RCA, CBS, the Times-Mirror Company, Gulf and Western, the Music Corporation of America, Time, Inc., and the New York Times. In 1977, the Literary Guild protested the "trend to concentration of power" in the book publishing industry claiming that of 1,200 book publishing companies, 63 firms produced two-thirds of the total (more than 200 titles each). It was also noted that the "big book" with huge promotion and profits was eclipsing smaller and perhaps better books, and that certain publishers and book clubs had an inside track to reviews in leading journals. All that looked grim. But offsetting such gigantism was noted a countertrend: proliferation of small, independent publishers ("funny little houses") that did add variety in publishing, even if that hope was dubious among the conglomerates (Loercher, 1978). It was noted that from 1958 to 1978 there had been an approximately 300 percent rise in the number of publishing companies (Robinson and Olszewski, 1980). And magazines, no longer primarily a mass medium (that function having been taken over by other media, especially television), were in larger proportions devoted to special interest audiences (Compaine, 1980).

Nor is the picture of concentration and loss of diversity in media all that different for the rest of the free world. Tunstall (1977) carried the charge of commercial domination worldwide, explaining how Anglo-American films, television, radio, news agencies, newspapers, and magazines, well made and high in cost, squeeze out local products that are at best poor imitations and make media dependent on advertising revenue—so helping turn the world into a sadly homogenized global village. Such Anglo-American domination of media in the free world is being counteracted by the Nonaligned News Agencies Pool, dedicated to two-way flow of information between developing and developed countries (Saranovic, 1978). Pool (1974), however, saw hope that domination by imported programs is only a temporary stage before people develop their own programming for indigenous values. We conclude that mass media have enormous potentiality for banalizing life as concentration and uniformity grow, even in a free market, but the balance and outcome are not yet clear.

We could not close this review of sources of cultural banality—however little our claim to cover everything—without some attention to loss of variety from overfiltering.

Many parts of culture—not just communication—filter information; over-filtering gives an experience of insipidity, or being cut off or sealed in. Three cases are blanding, effort-saving technology, and simulation of the real.

The filtering function of culture can be illustrated by sunglasses, window screens, cooking, and water purification systems. Even ideas and beliefs filter, as abstractions and as prejudices. Wisdom filters lessons from hard knocks. Indeed, the brain itself can be considered a filter and boredom a means by which it avoids information overload. Generally, a filter might be defined as any part of a system that cuts out unwanted variety. Beer's (1972:120) definition applies to communication: "We could define a filter as a many-one variety reducer. So a filter must either suppress some information, altogether, declaring it to be 'noise' (that is, irrelevant), or it must combine information in some way, so that only one thing is transmitted where more than one thing arrived."

It follows that trouble can arise if the filter cuts out variety we need and want. Cultural filtering is not always a good bargain. It can cut out characteristic tones until one can hardly tell one musical instrument from another. Even the telephone Jean Cocteau called "the most banal of modern inventions" because it cuts out visual images and many characteristics of the voice. Filtering is carried too far when information blocked out is more valuable than what comes through, as when news media are censored; or drinking water is so purified by distillation that it lacks not only germs but taste. Filtering goes awry when it leaves out so much of nature that a person feels sealed in, cut off, insipid, sterile, or fake.

The city easily gives the experience of being sealed in—by concrete, steel, glass, billboards, freeways, noise. A Londoner expresses such a feeling: "In the city one has the feeling of being in a comfortable cage, very ingeniously constructed, satisfactorily adjusted to all one's needs, but completely, or almost completely, insulated from the blustrous bonhomie of Nature" (Forbes-Boyd, 1978). Sociologist William Whyte (1980:74) describes urban megastructures:

Their enclosing walls are blank, windowless, and to the street they turn an almost solid face of concrete or brick.... One feels somewhat disembodied in these places. Is it night? Or day? Spring? Or Winter? And where are you? You cannot see out of the place. You do not know what city you are in, or if you are in a city at all.... The piped music gives no clue. It is the same as it is everywhere. ... You are in a universal controlled environment.

One can feel cut off or sealed in even in a suburb, with its newly planted trees, tidy lawns, and clean streets. And people themselves can give that feeling in "one-layer" communities, such as suburbs or mobile home parks, where there is only one kind of people who think and act pretty much alike. In such a case, the feeling is of a certain sterility.

Blanding is a plain example of over-filtering. It is a deliberate effort to remove strong tones or rough edges from experience to produce a more comfortable insipidity. In a pleasure-oriented society, merely to be comfortable is considered reason to euphemize, cosmetize, turn the tone dial to mellow, put happy endings on stories.

Food is a familiar example. Taking the hotness out of chili and curry and spice out of baby foods pleases those with tender palates. But as more foods are more blanded, people begin to complain that all foods taste the same and that it is impossible to get the "real thing."

Perhaps the main reason for blanding is to please the largest audience or market by avoiding unpleasantness to anybody. So products and messages are tailored to have no feature that might offend anyone. A literary classic like "The Merchant of Venice" might be laundered of some of Shylock's lines. Anxious parents and experts on children might propose to remove violence from fairy tales and Mother Goose—a proposal debated by Bruno Bettelheim, *The Uses of Enchantment* (1976), who argues that fairy stories confront the child's anxieties and support his sense of justice (evil deeds should be violently punished)—serving needs that cannot be met by bland, innocuous fiction. A federal agency charged with standardizing the nomenclature of maps, with typical bureaucratic timidity revised colorful but objectionable place names, such as Whorehouse Meadow to Naughty Girl Meadow, and Niggerhead Pond to Marshfield. Likewise, trying to please as many as possible and offend nobody adds to the tedium and evasive jargon of political speech making. But the larger the audience, the harder such a policy is to follow. Sooner or later, one is put into the predicament of the disc jockey who complained: "If you come on saying 'Happy Mother's Day,' someone will call in and ask, 'What's the matter, don't you like your father?' "

Wanting to be popular is an important reason for blanding. For the sake of popularity, people may smile all the time (a tactic first recommended by Dale Carnegie who wrote, "If you want people to like you ... smile"). They may change names like Doris von Kappelhoff to Doris Day, or Benny Kubelsky to Jack Benny. They may even use plastic surgery to turn "interesting" noses into standard profiles. On Madison Avenue, beauty is the "American look," which means Anglo-Saxon features— blond hair, blue eyes, a small nose, a big mouth, and on males, ears that do not stick too far out. A plastic surgeon complains, "What right do we have to apply Anglo-Saxon standards of beauty to everyone?" (Fenwick, 1979). Accent Therapists, a new industry in California, offers to launder speech of regional color, because without an accent people have "greater acceptability" (Maddocks, 1979). Status anxiety blands people, for they become ill at ease, too careful about how they look and act, suppressing natural impulses, acting by safe rules, nothing but clichés flow.

Sometimes technical factors cause blanding, as in televising orchestral music, where there are no peaks of volume because broadcast engineers equalize the intensities of loud and soft notes, making pianissimo and fortissimo identical (Patterson, 1974:95). But more often profitability from the largest audience or market seems the overriding motive. Harry Reasoner (1974) noted that for the sake of salability "Merry Christmas" on greeting cards was giving way to the more generalized "Season's Greetings." Cuteness is a highly salable form of blanding (Kewpie dolls, the large friendly eyes of Disney's Bambi. Norman Rockwell's pictures of puppy dogs, barefoot boys and gruff grandfathers provided covers for the *Saturday Evening Post* for many years, but by 1969 he said he was sick of it:

If a picture wasn't going very well I'd put a puppy dog in it, always a mongrel, you know, never one of the full bred puppies. And then I'd put a bandage on its foot. ... I was doing this "best of all possible worlds" kind of thing of Santa Clauses going up and down chimneys and lovely children adoring their kindly grandfathers. And I liked it when I did it, but now I'm sick of it. We've got sophisticated problems now (Omang, 1969).

In such ways, blanding, by reducing variety and taking rough edges off messages, produces noodles of communication. So it helps to make life more like a stainless steel tube through which people slide to destinations without hassle—yet with a feeling that something was missing along the way.

Adding to the smoothness of the ride through the tube are arrangements to lessen the effort of living. Wherever one looks, there seems almost to be a conspiracy to take away the experience of trying hard. Photoelectric eyes make it unnecessary even to push a button to get a door to open. Pushing a button on an electronic organ can make one an instant musician, with full harmonies and a rhythm accompaniment. Sports are becoming more and more a matter of what the *equipment* does than the person. Power toys take effort out of exercise. The Mayo Clinic's Dr. Gordon Martin commented, "Effortless exercise is about as meaningful as a foodless meal." Even schools (and perhaps this is a clue to their tedium) seem dedicated to making education as effortless as possible, whether by sheer inactivity (pupils sitting in classes where nothing is happening but someone talking), or by technological aids (television, computers, machine-scored examinations). A cartoon portrayed the ultimate in automatized education: an empty classroom in which tape recorders on students' desks were dutifully taking down a lecture from a machine on the teacher's desk—everyone apparently having found something better to do with his time.

All too often, the result of such effort saving is to deprive people of satisfying energetic outlets, to produce an imbalance between input and the personal output that gives life zest and meaning—not enough of what Czikszentmihalyi (1975) calls "flow." Media make passive audiences, taking everything in, denied the opportunity to be involved. It is not hard to imagine that many more effort-saving innovations could put modern people into a plight like that of a bed patient who can only close his eyes, look at the ceiling, switch television channels, or press a button for a nurse.

Another development of modern culture that gives a feeling of being sealed in is simulations and fakes so natural that one can hardly tell them from the real. Veneers, plastics, chemicals, photographs, holographs, lifelike robots and dummies, and other artificial substitutes seem to be taking over the environment. This is illustrated by an incident in Los Angeles during the 1960s. The city council tried lining a boulevard with plastic trees. At the time it seemed a sensible idea, for they saved water and looked just as good as living trees. But an unexpected public outcry forced the city to abandon the project. People expressed a peculiar horror at fake trees outdoors. They suggested that the entire environment could become artificial. Could the world turn into a sort of wax museum?

Such a fear is not unlike that felt by some musicians at electronic synthesizers, making sounds never produced by human hands or voices. A similar disquiet comes from unknowingly holding long correspondences with computers, and from telephone-answering devices that mimic familiar voices of the famous—John Wayne, Frank Sinatra, Johnny Cash—while telling the caller to leave his number.

The time may be coming when people prefer the fake to the real, even outdoors. Theodore Roszak (1972) tellingly noted that people have so come to expect the artificial that a boy watching Old Faithful geyser in Yellowstone Park was heard to remark, "Disneyland is better."

Already, one sees imitation places, such as a shopping center with nostalgia sprayed on by fake adobe and names like Ye Olde Butcher Shoppe and El Hombre Barbershop—perhaps a covered wagon parked outside. I am not talking about historical restorations such as Williamsburg, preserving what is left of the authentic, but places that are constructed like a movie set, pretending to be what they are not. Disney is the culture hero of such simulation. His enterprise boldly constructed fake historical places, such as Fort Wilderness campground; River Country with raft riding and log rolling; and Wilderness Swamp Trail, with canoeing, moonlight nature walk, and campfire with marshmallows and sing-along. According to Davis (1979:121), Disneyland and Disney World are "memory emporiums" in which visitors are "led back sentimentally to the small town atmosphere of America" at the turn of the century. Such myth making by media, says Davis, memorializes an "age of innocence" in which Americans feel they have lived because movies, stories, and radio serials have created a romanticized "secondhand reality," which is given a certain "credibility" by reminiscences from parents and grandparents.

Beyond fake memories is an entirely artificial community, an amusement park constructed as a place to live. One glimpse of such a world is Disney Enterprise's EPCOT (Experimental Prototype Community of Tomorrow) aiming to turn an amusement park into a "destination resort."

A further step toward an artificial world is capsules for living in outer space. Having their own recycled water and air, trees, soil, food, and simulated gravity, they will house colonies of thousands within the next few decades, according to planners such as Gerard K. O'Neill of Princeton University. Already volunteers are ready who say they will not miss the Earth but will be content to live within the artificial ecological system. Perhaps babies could be prepared for such a life by training in psychologist B.F. Skinner's famous box, a scientifically designed, glass-sided enclosure controlling the environment of an infant gurgling and crawling about within it. (The box aroused a furor which Skinner felt was unjustified, for it never was meant to be a substitute for natural life, only an experimental environment.)

A less reassuring picture of a sealed-in future comes from the imagination of writers like Samuel Beckett. His *The Lost Ones* (1972) depicts a rubber-like cylinder, 50 meters around and 18 high, in which dwell 200 men and women crowded one body per square meter. It is lit by a dim yellow light, the temperature fluctuating every four seconds between hot and cold in parody of an oscillating thermostat. Inmates roam in the gloom ceaselessly searching for lost ones, queuing at ladders which rise to niches and caves in the upper part; and wandering over the floor, which is divided into zones with complicated rules for movement. Seldom do mates find each other. Some huddle in positions of despair, "never again will they ceaselessly come and go who now at long intervals come to rest without ceasing to search with their eyes." Who are the lost ones? What does the cylinder represent? Beckett, as usual, does not tell. We are at liberty to guess that it is some faraway place, a desperate survival situation, a bomb shelter, a concentration camp, a mythical labyrinth like that of the Minotaur; or a life yet to come—or the life of almost any of us living in cities today.

Thus over-filtering may give us a bland, sterile world, in which culture separates us ever more from nature. More and more people may be so sealed in by artificiality, plastic, and effort-saving technology that they will, as Melvin Maddocks joked, find out what the weather is like by turning on the television instead of opening a window.

So we have looked at some sources of tiresome sameness in modern culture: substitution of mechanical for organic form, modernization and spread of popular at cost of indigenous culture, imitation of celebrity models, fashion redundancy, uniformity of media, and over-filtering. This excessive redundancy is one way in which information degrades, by saying again and again what may not have been interesting in the first place. So degrading, information gains entropy as we shall consider in Chapters 6, 7, and 9.

I make no claim to have covered all the sources of banality in modern culture, nor to have gotten them into proper perspective and proportion. But there seems little doubt that the sources are considerable. How strong a trend banalization is, and whether it will overcome more variety, are questions that remain unsettled.

But, in the light of many sources of redundancy, perhaps it is too soon to declare a victory for "demassification" by media and new technology giving more diversity of choice, as Toffler (1980) claims and Schrank (1977:64) denies.

Is diversity growing in book and magazine publishing? Are ethnic communities differentiating? Is there more variety on the leisure scene? Is there greater individualization of consumers' values, as shown by market research? Will new economic and communication technology add to variety of choice in such ways as customizing products; mini-markets; electronic cottage industries; flex-time; daily use of computers; mini-magazines carrying specialized messages to small segments of the public; tape recorders, video-cassettes, cable television, and personal and local publications, multiplying choices of channels and messages—all comprising a "third wave" that will make mass production, standardized living, and lack of fulfillment of the machine age obsolete, as Toffler predicts?

One hopes so. But it remains to be seen how they will work out in an interplay of forces. More need to be entered into the account before a balance can be reckoned.

Here even in banality we find something encouraging. If boredom creates a resistance—a defense—against more of that sort of information, wry comfort is to be found in the thought that, if media are doing the harm critics have feared, boredom generated by media redundancy will offset some of such bad effects. There is a good side to boredom if it immunizes us to pollution.

A fundamental question remains about redundancy, namely, what causes it to function well or poorly? Is it merely a matter of quantitative overload? What distinguishes "good" redundancy from banality? We shall try to answer this in the next chapter.

6

BAD VERSUS GOOD REDUNDANCY

"Thanks for the Memories"

—Bob Hope

Having attributed much of the boredom of modern life to banality, an overload of redundancy that makes experience insipid and the environment an emotional flatland, we note that there is another sort of redundancy with opposite effects.

This sort of redundancy is warm and meaningful, and absolutely essential for personal identity and social life. Unfortunately, redundancy is not always appreciated. People usually think of it as something you don't need, like a buggy whip or a fifth hand at bridge. Tell a man on the job he is redundant and he will expect to be fired. Redundancy so conceived is not even spare, like a fifth tire. It is useless—something to be thrown away.

But there is appreciation of some things of the past, provided one does not call them redundant: enthusiasm for souvenirs, heirlooms, and antiques; restoration of historic structures (Greiff, 1971); tracing genealogical "roots"; the extraordinary popularity of the television series "Upstairs, Downstairs" recalling Victorian ways—expressions of nostalgia (Davis, 1979). This sort of information repeats what has already been said, so it is redundant. But though repetitious, it is not felt as boring—quite the contrary. Let us call it (with apology for the subjectivity of the term) "good" redundancy.

Our purpose here, then, is to try to see better what "good" redundancy consists of; then how "bad" redundancy (banality) falls short—degrades into entropy. This comparison can be made on four points: how redundancy functions (or fails) to provide (1) continuity, (2) aid to communication, (3) identity, and (4) social resonance.

On the first point, since it repeats what has already been said or is already known, the message of redunancy is either to reveal a state of the past (as might a historical document), or to tell that "things are as they were"—friends remain friends, words mean the same, and the like. Far from being useless, such repetitive information is reassuring and helpful; it keeps our world going; without it, our thread of continuity would snap, individually and collectively. We need a continual bath of such reassurance. Perhaps the first human experience of "good" redundancy is the mother's heartbeat.

Emphasizing the importance of redundancy, Bateson (1972:415) defines it so broadly as to take in all predictability or patterning in the environment or in signals animals make. The goal of information is to create redundancy, that is, pattern, order, out of variety (pp. 130–131). In this broad sense, redundancy is no less than the lawfulness of the universe, on which we count if we know its signs, to go on doing things in the same old way. The social function of redundancy for continuity, then, is to surround us with familiar cues assuring us that things are, and will continue to be, what they seem; that people are known and reliable; that debts will be paid, money is good, and so on. Our social world in this sense *is* redundancy, which is about synonymous with culture. So redundancy is a conserving mechanism, what William James called the great flywheel of habit that keeps society going.

Classic literature and art—as distinguished from news and the latest technical information and popular culture—preserve cherished values of the past and so serve continuity.

Ritual forms and language also serve social continuity. If one thinks of ritual as some kind of rigamarole, magic or pompous fanfare, then one belittles it; but if one thinks of it as a language then one more easily argues its importance as redundancy for society, its function being to preserve and restate certain nondiscursive themes of meaning. Though one cannot translate, it is possible to summarize, however inadequately, themes of ritual important in almost all groups, though the forms of expression vary. We might paraphrase some typical messages: (1) "You are not alone. We are all together"—the ritual of solidarity, fellowship, belongingness, esprit de corps; (2) "Do not worry. Things will work out all right. Something you do not understand is working for you"—a language of reassurance, found often in white magic; (3) "Congratulations, you made the grade"—the rites of status transition; (4) "We hold this to be right and self-evident"—moral affirmation; (5) "Crime does not pay"—the ill-doer gets what he deserves—dramatization of moral debt and punishment, the theme of morality plays, crime dramas, horse opera, court ceremony, and sorcery for law enforcement in primitive societies; (6) "That is ridiculous. Don't be a jerk. Don't do it"—negative models and comic justice in clowning, burlesque, satire; (7) "I owe you, you owe me"—the ritual of reciprocity; (8) "We are like brothers"—the ritual of kinship extension; (9) "Honestly, I'll really try. I'll never quit"—oaths and resolutions which bind a person to a path or obligation; (10) "Help us, Supreme Power, don't harm us"—the ritual of propitiation and penance; (11) "We are cleansed, redeemed, born again"—the ritual of purification; (12) "Aren't we proud of ourselves!"—the ritual of pomp. Without presuming to exhaust them, I think we can see that such messages and mystiques are too much for mere verbal statement and too important to leave to chance. Groups take every opportunity to emphasize them by emotional ceremonies (Klapp, 1969:120–121). Once seen as such language, there is little argument about the importance of ritual (and its redundancy) for society, since it helps people to feel more together—solidarity and fullness of emotional life being two important consequences of communicating by ritual. For societies it means maintaining sentiments necessary for social structures, as explained by Durkheim, Radcliffe-Brown, and anthropologists and sociologists following them.

Within the historical time dimension, redundancy provides service to continuity by recycling information from the past back into the present circuit: from memory (and the genetic codes) into decision and learning; and from generation to generation as culture. Such redundancy is like money in the bank: symbolic capital.

On the second score, redundancy aids communication in many ways, whether by repeating information within a message or series of messages coming from several channels, or cues in the context telling us what we may assume about the source and intention of the message. So redundancy serves as a kind of insurance for messages: that they will not be lost or misunderstood, or the memory tape erased. It may be deliberately added to messages to overcome error and noise, as when a check states the number of dollars as well as the word for that number. Because we usually do not need all of this repetition, it is in fact useless much of the time. If our memory is good, we do not need a grocery list, still less a reminding call from our wife. The more careless and noisy communication is, the more redundancy is needed; J.R. Pierce (1961:143) says, "It is only because of redundancy that anyone can read my hand-writing." A general rule is that the more likely a signal is to be lost, faded, garbled, or misunderstood, the more it should be repeated and amplified. Redundancy can also be increased by multiplying channels or preestablishing understandings about the message. Much of our knowl-edge of English grammar and spelling is built in so that we need not discuss it with other English speakers; indeed, Birdwhistell (1970) says that without such internalized automatic rules we could not communicate by language at all. It is widely agreed that most languages have about 50 percent redundancy; perhaps this is an ideal mix for life in general, speculates Colby (1958). By such services to communication, redundancy makes messages more widely available in a population, so contributing to viability of a species, says Birdwhistell. Nor need we play down the role of colloquialisms—clichés, slogans, aphorisms, jokes, even stereo-types—in making person-to-person understanding quicker. Even in art, for all its search for the new, says Anton Ehrenzweig (1970), the de-struction of cliché and convention would at some point mean loss of ability to communicate—or to create. Especially in music and the lively arts redundancy helps resonance. What, for example, would Ravel's "Bolero" be if its length were reduced by half? In sum, redundancy seems as important to communication as is new information. Without either, there is no message.

On the third score is the service of redundancy to identity, personal and collective. Everyone knows the good feeling that comes from contact with an important part of one's past—photo albums, school yearbooks, remembering good times together, reunions, candles on a cake, a letter to a teacher from a student who remembers her, familiar places revisited. Such things bring back warm memories and sentiments. Popular or-chestras keep a "memory book" of tunes likely to be requested by sectors of the audience. Such tunes invite people to recall how it was to be young then. When listening to the songs of one's own place and vintage, one has the feeling of being restored to oneself, alive again in a time when perhaps one was most alive. Fortunately, there are over-lapping bands of memory, maybe folk songs or classics, in which all of the audience can join. That good feeling comes from redundancy as the capacity of symbols to give us back part of ourselves. Good redundancy warms the heart, restores us, gives us something we need, makes us whole, tells us who we are and were. Conversely, its loss is really an identity problem—without it we cannot fully appreciate who we are or have continuity as persons. Souvenirs supply memory, and memory of "who I was at all preceding moments" becomes "who I am." In this sense, identity is the staked out, recallable, reclaimable part of our stream of experience. To lose all of the past, as in amnesia, would be to lose ourselves. Souvenirs and ceremonies earmark certain parts of the past as especially memorable, to be recalled as needed. Only in its capacity to be replayed as part of the self does any information serve identity as the concept of who we are. Otherwise it merely enters the stream of forgotten experience. So, good redundancy is the stuff of personal identity, information about the kind of person we were played back to us for us to decide either to go on doing the same thing or to do something different. In short, redundancy feels good when it has the capacity to give us back part of ourselves and to restore meaning to us.

Much the same is true of the service of redundancy to collective identity, except that the ceremonies and memories are more public and concern the concept of "we" more than "I." A calendar of anniversaries and holidays outlines a machinery for recalling collective identity, whether of family, church, corporation, tribe, or nation.

On the fourth score is the function of good redundancy for resonance, attunement, and warm responsiveness in human relations (referred to variously as sympathy, empathy, camaraderie, "we" feeling, esprit de corps, affinity, rapport, being "on the same wavelength," seeing eye-to-eye, being engrossed, "warming up to," "turned on," swinging, "good vibes"). Feeling so attuned, many things are possible in human relations that would not be so if relations are formal or cool.

Resonance is response to others with a feeling of active engagement, attunement, "swinging" as it is sometimes described. A familiar example of lack of resonance is the lady who, after a jazz concert, said, "I did not tap my foot." She was complaining that the music did not reach her with melodies, harmonies and rhythms that she knew and liked enough to join in. She could not resonate and was bored. Lack of resonance makes experience dull, flat, and "objective." Instead of engaging, an audience merely sits and watches. Resonance is based on attunement of parties to a certain "wavelength." It is not mere arousal (you can be aroused by an earthquake but not attuned to one). Very often modern art and music suffer from lack of resonance because striving for originality they try to be all surprise, and so neglect the redundancy—the common band of familiarity—that is necessary for resonance and even meaning to the audience.

To feel attuned requires that people be able to replay bands of redundancy that match with each other's memories, language, songs, dance
steps, anecdotes, and so on. Familiar information has one capacity that
the unfamiliar cannot have: to call one into a performance that matches
the pattern or rhythm of another in a nicely responsive way. In music
and the lively arts, redundancy in forms like rhythm and repeating themes
helps resonance. Resonance is manifested by such things as tapping one's
foot with the beat, moving one's body empathetically while watching a
sport or dance, hearing an old joke and being ready to laugh at the
punch line because one knows what is coming. The good feeling comes
from putting ourselves in, responsively vibrating in heart or body because
we, too, know how and like to do it. Such responsiveness and togetherness can come only from information that is redundant in ways just
described. Variety—totally new experience—can produce arousal but
not resonance (in the physical analogy, the violin or piano string vibrates
at the *same* pitch as one—not all—the musical notes sung or played
nearby).

So far, we have distinguished four functions of good redundancy:
continuity, communication, identity, and social resonance. Because of
such functions, good redundancy feels good when experienced, hurts
when lost; warms the heart, gives something we need; restores part of
ourselves, makes us whole, reinforces identity; and brings people closer
through resonance.

Humans have far greater capacity for resonance than, say, a radio but
can also fail to resonate in more ways. Indeed, resonance is a quality
often lacking in the impersonality and formalism of modern life. When
these functions fail, it seems we get a redundancy that is sterile, restrictive, and boring. Let us try to see of what this difference consists and,
if possible, hypothesize about what causes redundancy to degrade (having
no empirical findings such as from experiments to test such hypotheses
but only preliminary induction from a few cases).

Let us proceed to define bad redundancy as having features opposite
to those of good redundancy: (1) If good redundancy serves social and
personal continuity, then bad redundancy weakens or disrupts it. This
seems to apply to the transiency of fads and fashions that, however
imitated, give no assurance that "things are as they were." Likewise it
applies to aspects of modernization, such as technology, mass-produced
commodities, and the displacement of indigenous by popular culture,
mentioned in Chapter 3. Likewise for media output that, however re-

petitive, has no historical roots or significance, no sense of something handed down. A television commercial, a rhetorical political appeal, a folksy show, an amusement park, can fool people by pretending to be good redundancy (connecting us with times past). Meanwhile, nostalgia hankers for a real past.

As to ritual, a prime servant of social continuity, the modern scene seems to be one of poverty of ritual (Klapp, 1969:126–137), in which, for example, bureaucratic procedures replace ceremonies such as college graduation; and genuine, meaningful ritual has deteriorated into that of the hollow sort called ritualism (or by Cooley, formalism), of which commercialized Christmas or the half-time celebrations at football games will serve as examples. We note also the function of shows like musical comedies, horse operas, soap operas, and television evangelism to compensate for an emotional emptiness that is due to the failure of institutions such as the family, and, in part, to the poverty of what ritual (however much of it) there is. The plight of much modern ritual—unless it is put on as entertainment—is to be boring, and to provide no more social and personal continuity than do the shows with which it competes. How meaningful ritual degrades into bad redundancy and how to create new ritual that will last as good redundancy, are problems yet to be solved.

(2) If good redundancy helps communication, then bad redundancy hinders it. In the simplest case, it is apparent that sheer amount of redundancy could take up so much channel time that little fresh information could come through. This is notably true of clichés and social roles that are like a mask, keeping people from getting really in touch with one another. Should one seek to establish resonance by clichés, very likely it does not come off, for neither party puts his heart into it—recognizes the cliché as his own with that good feeling of identity restored. It applies also to impersonal messages from media, which give no assurance that we are really in touch with anyone, especially when the medium reveals (as in the case of computers and answering devices) that nobody is even there at the other end of the line. In the same way, Jean Renoir (1974) distinguishes the message of craftsmanship from that of mass production:

Everything made by hand is like a message from its maker, it contains life. What difference does it make if the design of a mass-produced plate is the work of a master?—the monotony of its mass-production induces a feeling of sadness, whereas the variety and imperfections of primitive utensils bring lightness of heart.

The "lightness of heart" comes from the assurance that someone is at the other end of the line, who has something to say to us, even whose mistakes are interesting. "Canned applause" is yet another example of the lack of message of bad redundancy: responding insensately during pauses in radio and television performances, it supplies no real feedback to performers. "The laugh track is killing comedy," remarked playwright Neil Simon, "because you don't have to be funny any more." "Dead audiences laughing at dead material," concurred television host Dick Cavett (Cavett, 1979). So redundancy that keeps information from coming through acts like a bad filter. As an ingredient of communication, it is sterile, inert, and uncommunicative, like paraffin in gasoline, having no message, so to speak, to the engine.

(3) On the score of identity, if good redundancy reinforces identity, then bad redundancy weakens it. Modernization, large-scale technology, bureaucracy, and pop culture, attenuate indigenous culture and identity. Fashions, although beginning as a statement of identity, drown in their own redundancy. Suburban development, making places seem alike, destroys their identity—as Gertrude Stein put it, "There's no there there." The point is that much redundancy, though diffused and in that sense shared, does not belong to any particular person or group. Nor can claiming it declare identity of anyone in particular. Like a cap or sweatshirt imprinted with a trademark like "Pepsi," wearing it does not bestow identity on those who are neither shareholders nor employees of that corporation. Such redundancy makes people more alike without giving them a sharper sense of who they are or a bond of solidarity (in Durkheim's terminology: a mechanical solidarity that is without cohesion— the solidarity of the crowd rather than of the tribe).

(4) If good redundancy supports resonance, then bad redundancy damps it. Unvarying repetition interferes with attunement in human relations. An example is found in the metronome, whose unvarying repetition of the same tempo helps the musician, but also arouses a well-known feeling of impatience if one has to play with the metronome very long. The reason for this is that exact mechanical regularity, while welcome as information for setting a tempo, soon becomes restrictive—a denial of information—when it keeps one from finding a better tempo, and lacks the liveliness of beat—even variations of tempo—of a real

drummer, telling that somebody is there. Likewise the mechanical vibrato of electronic instruments is lifeless compared with a humanly produced vibrato. Musicians can tell mechanical from humanly produced music by lack of inflection and microvariations in the former. A modern composer, Steve Reich, explained why he doesn't like the sound of synthesizers. As with the metronome, it is the absence of lively variations:

Take a synthesized tone, run it into an oscilloscope, and you'll see a steady wave form on the screen. But ask a violinist to play the same note similarly—with no vibrato and no inflection whatsoever—and you'll see the tone on the oscilloscope dancing and jumping all over the place! Now go into the room blindfolded. In about three seconds you can *hear* and *feel* that it's live music. It's that micro-variation in a "perfect" ensemble that gives the music its life (Sterritt, 1980).

Such unvarying unresponsiveness seems to epitomize the effect of banality in society, the difficulty in attunement found in any relationship that is mechanical, formalistic, or bureaucratic and ignores individual variations. It is felt by a student taking a machine-scored examination that has no space for his thoughts, or a customer billed by a computer. The time has arrived, however, when computers are approaching the borderline at which they seem lively and human. Some can utter and answer human speech, even talk on the phone with automatic dialing systems and pre-recorded questions or sales pitches, capable of making a thousand calls a day to homeowners surprised to find they have talked to a computer on the other end of the line. A computer can also simulate a psychiatric interview and play psychiatrist with a human patient by being programmed to respond to key words like "father," "unhappy," with general answers that produce a conversation seemingly as coherent as most real ones (which also have a high level of redundancy and irrelevance). Does this mean that machines are becoming less redundant in their output, or that clichés of real life are not all that different from those of a machine?

At any rate, whether with machines or people, failure to sustain resonance seems to be a chief mark by which we recognize bad redundancy. We become aware that it has little to say: that it depresses the alert give-and-take that makes life interesting—that exact repetition cuts off all the other things that might have been said, such as how people really feel—that it is indifferent and does not respond to our needs.

But much of the time, without our recognizing it, banality comfortably encloses us in small talk, soft canned music, vapid speeches, political clichés, complacent clatter, push-button living, monotonous stimuli of one kind or another. Lacking surprise or enigma to challenge curiosity, the situation becomes flat and is perceived indifferently because nothing is expected. But when banality is felt as a denial of information, it arouses boredom.

In short, bad redundancy is a lack of information which, degraded, cheats in some way. It filters out some needed parts of a message while repeating too much that is not needed. It does not restore the past, roots, or anything else, so that it fails to serve continuity. It does not reinforce identity. It chills relationships and defeats resonance. Failing to give what we want, it is felt as boring, cold, shallow, versus the warm and deep feeling of good redundancy.

We have looked at a few cases of bad redundancy, trying to see what distinguishes it from good redundancy. Losing functions for continuity, communication, identity, and social resonance, redundancy turns into clutter, junk.

With more and more information pouring upon us, it will become more important to understand what—besides sheer repetition—makes information lose functions of good redundancy and become banal and boring. The quality of life, if not our very continuity and identity, may depend on it.

I readily admit having done no more than pose the problem of what makes good redundancy turn into bad—why does it degrade? Is it an expression of entropy, paralleling noise in channels?

The most apparent hypothesis is that any insertion of an unvarying or mechanical-seeming element into a living system or process (suppose in a mosque a recorded voice instead of a live muezzin calls Muslims to prayer) increases banality and boredom. Perhaps such a hypothesis could be tested in various church, ceremonial, entertainment, and educational settings.

As the matter now seems to stand, modern society—without taking much account of such things—is oscillating between overloads of banality on one hand, and noise on the other.

Let us look at the other extreme in the next two chapters.

7

WHEN INFORMATION TURNS TO NOISE

We have been looking at a degradation of information called banality, a sort of creeping sameness. But that is only part of the picture. Variety, also, can be boring when it has nothing to say—when it inflicts on us noise, distraction and irrelevance, making it harder to find the meaning we seek. Nor dare we assume that the slow pace of country life is more boring than the city, with all its sights, noise, and excitement, for each has its own boringness. There is tedium on a country road on which few vehicles pass, but there is also tedium on a highway on which hundreds of vehicles pass in an hour. There is tedium of working alone on a farm, but there is tedium also in greeting hundreds of strangers in a reception line. There is tedium of shopping in a store that handles only a few kinds of merchandise, but there is also tedium (rather like museum fatigue) from shopping in a department store that sells thousands of different things. The important question is, what is the chance of *significant* information, whether from redundancy or variety.

Without significance, variety is not the spice of life. It can be as dull as monotony when it has nothing to say—becomes noiselike. Information theory helps explain how variation as it approaches randomness loses meaning and seems all the same. J.R. Pierce (1961:267) says all completely random (Gaussian) noise sounds alike, hence unsurprising, monotonous, even if it is most various and unpredictable. This is because to recognize a thing as new, one must be able to distinguish it from what is old. But, to be distinguishable, some of the things we perceive must be similar enough as classes or patterns for us to compare with another thing to tell if it is the same or different. So unfamiliar languages and music (such as rock, jazz and flamenco) sound "all the same" to the uninitiated. Pierce says, "To be appreciated art must be in a language familiar to the audience; otherwise no matter how great the variety may be, the audience

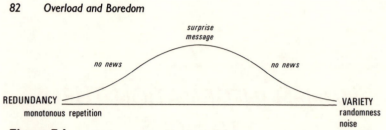

Figure 7.1

Loss of Communication at Extremes of Redundancy and Variety

will have an impression of monotony or sameness. We can be surprised repeatedly only by contrast with that which is familiar, not by chaos." Music develops by variation *upon* a theme; there cannot be significant variation without a theme.

A similar point is made by E. H. Gombrich (1979:104–111) applying information theory to perception of art. Perception does not work like a camera; it is selectively focused on redundancy (pattern, continuity) or surprise of discontinuity. Discontinuity has an alerting effect. "Disturbance of regularity, such as a flaw in a smooth fabric, can act like a magnet to the eye, and so can an unexpected regularity in a random environment such as the mysterious fairy rings in wild woodlands" (p. 122). Both continuity and discontinuity are necessary for art to be interesting. If pattern is lacking and all is random, attention quits for the same reason as when all is redundant: no surprise.

From this we see that wearisome sameness in modern life could not all be attributed to uniformity, if so much of it comes also from meaningless variety. Perhaps it would be better, then, to think of information poverty as a small chance of significant information, whether from uniformity or variety. This takes us further in understanding the high level of boredom in modern society in spite—possibly on account—of all its variety and change. Understanding that a large part of the information of modern life has a random, irrelevant, even chaotic character, we see that lack of meaning lies at both ends of the continuum from redundancy to variety. Too far either way spells boredom.

Figure 7.1 shows how communication could fail to deliver information (surprise), from extremes either of redundancy or variety. One cannot be surprised if things are all the same, or all different. Entropy, as loss of meaning, always lurks at both ends of the continuum from banality to noise.

This dilemma, as it often proves to be, between redundancy and variety, is illustrated by creative artists—in painting, Jackson Pollack—in music, Igor Stravinsky, Charles Ives, and Arnold Schönberg—who, in their eagerness to avoid the trite and say something new, veer dangerously into randomness and dissonance that sound like noise to the less adventurous. A critic (Owens, 1982) says of Schönberg:

Key centers were not just evaded, their very existence was denied in a technique which used combinations (rows) of the twelve chromatic tones. They were all used as equals, and none might be repeated until all the others had been sounded. ... The rule was supposed to banish any hints of tonality.... But what is very plainly missing is an equally compelling set of tonal reasons for what is going on.

Schönberg's rule, and avoiding frequencies between the tones, provided some redundancy, which kept his compositions from otherwise possibly being sheer noise. It remains true that an art which approaches noise too closely may destroy itself.

So (signaling poor information) boredom lies at both ends of the continuum from redundancy to variety shown in Figure 7.1. This reflects the paradox of boredom from too much, as from too little, variety.

The meaning-defeating (boring) element in variety is commonly called noise. We are reminded of how very noisy our society is by such things as ceaseless roar of traffic, blast of jets, television commercials, and people on the street carrying cassette recorders blaring out rock to passers-by. Most people regard noise as a trivial, if bothersome, acoustical by-product of technology. But there is more to it if one sees that many sorts of noise impair communication and meaning—the more noise, the less meaning; by generating so much noise, modern society loses some meaning.

To look further into this, it is important to define noise and distinguish noisy from useful information, since information is not inherently different from noise. It depends on how communication—what is coming through a channel—*acts*, and on whom. Ashby (1956:186) says:

It must be noticed that noise is in no intrinsic way distinguishable from any other form of variety. Only when some recipient is given, who will state which of the two is important to him, is a distinction between message and noise possible. ... "Noise" ... is ... purely relative to some given recipient, who must say which information he wants to ignore.

We quickly recognize as noise a racket or chatter interfering with the signal we want (or disturbing the quiet that is a condition for receiving the signal). But noise need not be senseless; perfectly good information, even an organized message, can act like noise when it interferes with or disturbs reception of some signal. Signals themselves can act as noise to other signals. So I would define noise as anything coming within a channel—signal or not—that disturbs or interferes with the signal the receiver is seeking. In this sense, perfectly good information can act as noise, if it is jumbled, irrelevant, or distracting, or its signal is so amplified (din, racket, clamor) that it drowns out a desired signal.

Yet, though noise can consist of signals meaningful to somebody, their impact on the receiver usually seems random, patternless, and senseless—they have no message for *him*. So it cannot be denied that, even when measured in decibels, noise is subjective, depending on receiver's taste, perception, intention, or expectation (expressed in the saying, "One man's music is another's noise," or the term noise used as an antonym of beauty). But subjectivity does not diminish its reality as a phenomenon.

But there is more to noise than meets the ear. It has a spectrum broader than auditory, and can occur in any sensory or symbolic mode— indeed, in any channel of any sort of information. In this broad sense, noise might occur anywhere that information is communicated, such as radio static, computer garbage, headlight glare, specks that spoil a photographic negative, typographical errors, distortion of rumors, genetic noise, interference between brain hemispheres, and so on. In this broad sense, noise is a concept fundamental for analysis of all biological and social systems as well as of information technology—a communicational form of entropy, intruding into and degrading information, at the human level opposed to meaning by its randomness and lack of message.

Sheer noise (random, senseless variety) is boring because it has no message. But more important for the modern information society is the huge amount of communication that carries clear messages yet is acting like noise on audiences and boring for that reason. How can information act like noise?

The average person may feel well informed, with news media keeping him posted hourly about world events, advertising pumping sales pitches at him, junk mail piling at the door, and magazines and books in drugstores and supermarkets as well as libraries and schools. But that feeling may be an illusion if most of the information is so poor in quality and so random as to be noiselike and very little is an answer to any question asked.

We do not judge the quality of information by its accuracy and clarity alone, but how it *acts* upon receivers, for example, whether it is useful and relevant, whether it is feedback to the receiver's question, whether it has much meaning or is merely a lot of facts, or, in terms of our theory, whether it is acting as noise or banality. As noise increases, it obstructs or interferes with meaning, therefore produces boredom as restlessness from perception of a small chance of learning anything interesting.

It is an irony of the information society that information gets in its own way—or, as one might put it, communication becomes noise to its own signal.

This can happen in various ways, such as: (1) loudness, (2) disconnectedness, (3) bad complexity, (4) decoding difficulty, (5) clutter of communication, 6) lack of feedback, 7) stylistic noise, (8) pseudo-information, and (9) sheer overload.

LOUDNESS, CLAMOR

Sheer loudness makes any signal noisy because, whether information or nonsense, its strength drowns out other stimuli that might be signals. Today competition to be heard so adds to the stridency and amplification of entertainment, advertising, and political messages that each is many times louder than necessary to be audible were it not for the others. Amplification of voices and musical instruments puts almost anybody "on the air"; even portable radios and cassettes can be used in public places as a sort of personal broadcasting. But loudness is not merely a matter of decibels; it can occur in other sensory modalities, as in a 20 foot-high billboard above smaller ones, blinking lights, searchlights, sky-writing, roadside kitsch (not excluding some public art), or a certain style or color that is said to be "loud" (meaning, perhaps, that it steals attention from quieter styles and colors). Noise will always denote that which makes the most clamor with the least message. Clamor arouses us to expect much, but in the case of noise its arousal is a false promise.

Intrusiveness describes the power of communication to penetrate our defenses and reach us whether we like it or not. What was called the jukebox problem in the 1930s has grown into a pervasive feature of modern life. Almost everyone has equipment by which to thrust tastes upon others, whether at home or at beaches and public parks.

Advertising is perhaps the most intrusive form of public communication. According to the American Association of Advertising Agencies, 1,600 commercial messages a day are directed at the average individual, of which we consciously notice 80. The main purpose of advertising is to implant unwanted messages into people. To do this an advertiser may spend a $1 millon for a minute of prime television time, which gives access to perhaps 50,000,000 minds. TV "clutter" (as the industry calls the noisy blur of commercials and announcements that interrupt programs continually) is designed to be intrusive, strident, even irritating, to penetrate whatever defenses audiences may have and implant a message before they can switch off. Polls show a majority of the TV audience dislikes interruption by commercials, and would be willing to pay for entertainment without them (ABC Report, March 18, 1979). "Junk mail" fills people's mailboxes (one housewife, saving such mail for a year, found it weighed 55 pounds). More intrusive is the hired telephone caller who chooses dinnertime to tell you of the advantages of an insurance policy. Fairly appalling is the thought that computer phone banks, instead of live people, can deliver 9,000 "personalized" calls per day into the home. Such intrusive communication—especially when it uses hidden persuaders (Packard, 1957; Key, 1973), subliminal perception (Dixon, 1971), and hypnosis—puts us in a predicament in which our mind is like an open tape recorder into which tracks are being inserted without our knowing it. In some ways, the mind is an almost nakedly open receptor. The neurosurgeon Wilder Penfield (1952:179, 188) found that our unconscious minds are incredible storehouses of practically everything that we have experienced; stimulating the brain with an electrode, he produced total playbacks, such as a musical performance heard at age five. Suppose one went about in public for 24 hours with a tape recorder switched on, taking in everything—traffic noises, trivial talk, other people's conversations. Imagine how it would sound in playback, in what state the tape message would be. Unless information is unconsciously being sorted into patterns higher than memory packages of uninterpreted experience, the mind might become like a garbage can. The individual is in the dilemma of the unguarded input: consciously stretching out antennae to hear what he needs, but constantly intruded by what he does not want (for example, he must listen to all the traffic noise for the screech of wheels that can make him jump, because if he doesn't, he will not hear the message that saves his life). A result of all this intrusiveness is that, alongside the slogans of "access to information" and "the right to communicate" of a free society, there begins to be a new emphasis on the right *not* to communicate and *not* to be communicated to—to disconnect, to switch off—and the need for laws to provide safeguards to protect individuals against invasions of personal privacy (Gotlieb and Gwyn, 1972).

At the international level, a similar problem is posed by direct satellite television broadcasting: the possibility of flooding countries by propaganda or cultural values beamed directly into them without consent. The dispute has been carried on since 1972 in the United Nations Working Group on Direct Broadcast Satellites. The main issue was not quality but "foreignness" of programs felt as threat to national culture. Third World countries complain of domination by Anglo-American media (Tunstall, 1977) and want their own news services. So intrusiveness of communication aggravates noise, violating boundaries, personal and cultural, increasing the sense of irrelevance, making whatever incongruity there may be in thought wildly, even painfully, so. At its worst it adds offense of bad taste, stylistic noise, information pollution, and the like (Klapp, 1978:4). There seems to be a sort of Gresham's Law favoring the loud.

DECODING DIFFICULTY

Jargon adds to the noiselike quality of information. The very word connotes a strange, barbaric tongue—"talk that is both ugly-sounding and hard to understand" (Fowler, 1974:315). Our world is filled with jargons that baffle understanding (computerese, bureaucratese, legaleze, gobbledegook, bafflegab, "psychobabble," and so on). Such jargons make even one's own language seem a Babel. While jargon may serve specialists, it makes language noisier—and more boring—to almost everybody else. While grammarians unite in deploring jargon, no one seems able to prevent it from displacing plain speech by a sort of Gresham's Law.

The noisiness of jargon is not so much its ugly sound as excessive difficulty in decoding. Ciphers are, one might say, a deliberately contrived noise (scrambling) to hide a signal, which deciphering overcomes. Past a point, decoding difficulty makes any communication noiselike, if the code acts more like a cipher than a signal; and the work of deciphering *ipso facto* carries no desired information and preoccupies the receiver at cost of other things he might have learned during the same time. Ambiguity and equivocation act as semantic noise because they add to the uncertainty of receivers as to which meaning was sent, and to the work of decoding, to say nothing of giving negative information (Harary and Batell, 1978) if the wrong meaning is chosen.

Besides, today so many more signals are exogenous—not immediately understood, but strange in origin, referring to things with which one has had little direct experience, coming from people one does not know; requiring continual definition, calculation, and testing, if one is to know what to make of them—that people carry a heavy burden of decoding, to which argots, jargons, neologisms, and vogue words add.

That growing difficulty of decoding—from such things as jargon, ambiguity, and exogenous signals—is more serious than mere inconvenience will be appreciated if we recall that coding is the hinge on which the door of communication swings freely—or creaks and sticks. That is, everything that communication does for our society, from the talk of neighbors to international diplomacy, is impaired by coding difficulty, not to enlarge upon the boredom it produces in education.

DISCONNECTEDNESS AND IRRELEVANCE

A third way in which information becomes noiselike is lack of apparent relation to other information with which the receiver is concerned: irrelevance or disconnectedness makes it harder to find a pattern (what Alfred North Whitehead called the "fatal disconnectedness" of subjects in education). When information is too disconnected, finding its meaning becomes like a gigantic, endless jigsaw puzzle of which the pieces do not fit. The modern person is faced with an ever-mounting heap of information that is likely to be out of place or context and in no apparent sequence. This disconnectedness puts us in a position like that of an archaeologist sorting shards from different strata trying to find another bit that matches. Irrelevance—lack of possible logical connection with a given topic—is especially hard to bear, because it frustrates meaning and is a strongly aversive kind of conceptual dissonance (Berlyne, 1960:288). A university student newspaper expresses such frustration:

What is wrong with the world today? In a word, boredom. How can that be, you may ask, in this fast paced kaleidoscope of a world that we live in.... Television and the other media have brought the world into our homes. This makes for a collage. The collage, however, has very little pattern to it or anything for that matter holding it together. We watch a movie and a commercial comes on for toothpaste, followed closely by one for hair cream, followed by toilet paper and finally back to the commercial, I mean movie. No reason behind all this, nothing. News story after news story greets us.... Naturally we get bored.

The trouble with news, according to James Carey (1969:35) is that, coming from various sources, it lacks a common perspective as to what is real and meaningful: " 'Objective reporting' does little more than convey this disorder in isolated, fragmented, news stories." The disorderliness of news is heightened by sensationalism. When the heap of knowledge is so huge, fragmented, and specialized, it seems almost a matter of arithmetic that there is an ever smaller chance that any bit will be relevant to a particular person, who must, even with the best intentions, spend much time being bored by topics about which he neither knows nor cares.

A powerful source of disconnectedness of information from meaning is separation of facts from values by positivistic science seeking value-free, objective knowledge—deplored by humanists such as Krutsch (1954), Maslow (1971), and Roszak (1972). Such a flood of disconnected bits is a threat to human dignity and autonomy, according to Karl Deutsch (1966:131–132, 240–241). On the other hand, Marshall McLuhan (1968) saw in it a challenge obliging readers and viewers to create their own connections. In either case, however, it means considerable work sorting and decoding information most of which is trivial, meaningless, or irrelevant.

Information about which one can do nothing (instruction without practice, passive entertainment without active play) adds to boredom and "learned helplessness" in television viewers unable to do anything about what they see. A content analysis of two weeks of NBC and CBS newscasts, rating items on a five-point "helplessness" scale, found that 71.4 percent of the time some degree of helplessness was displayed, averaging "between mild and moderate, closer indeed to moderate" (Levine, 1977).

Transience and decay of media messages add another dimension to degradation of information. As is well known, most messages from television, films, radio, newspapers, and magazines are consumed quickly and then perish. Their short life span emphasizes "timeliness, superficiality, or sensationalism in what is fundamentally a one-time chance to attract large audiences." Fleetingness lessens the ability of the audience to comprehend messages. However, video cassette recorders somewhat offset transiency by allowing a second look or hearing and make it possible to save some otherwise unrepeated TV programs and so reduce the rate of decay (Levy and Fink, 1984). Transiency also characterizes fads, which, rapidly adopted, exhaust the market by redundancy and satiation, so that their value falls precipitously. It is evident that the faster messages and fads decay and the more disconnected they are, the less durably meaningful and more noiselike such information is in retrospect.

It is difficult to separate disconnectedness of information from a characteristic of our society that I call bad complexity.

BAD COMPLEXITY

Complexity is often held to be more interesting than simplicity, because it has more to reveal; yet there is a boring and frustrating kind, of which our society is full. Bad complexity contains maximum disorder, expressed by names like jumble, hodgepodge, clutter, tangle, snarl. One finds it in a jumbled set of printer's type or a tangled fishing line ("bird's nest"), which gives no inherent satisfaction in disentangling, nor would one put it in a box and give it as a puzzle. Other names for bad complexity are red tape, proliferation, sprawl, complication, contraption. One might call it complicatedness to distinguish it from good complexity. Many institutions merit comparison with a Rube Goldberg contraption (that humorous assemblage of incongruous components hitched together by improvisation, which, if it works at all, will seem a miracle). "The present government involvement in the operation of the United States economy presents a confusing picture of a sprawling labyrinth rather than a blueprint of a rationally designed edifice," said Wassily Leontief (Leontief, 1982). Good complexity has pattern that is intelligible and often pleasing to the human mind—a signal that we can hope to understand and manage it. Instead of such information, bad complexity has an element of confusion (tangledness, clutter, and so on) that baffles the mind because it has no pattern that can serve as a key by which to unravel, decipher, or manage it. Confusion and clutter are signs of entropy, useless disorder that on the communicational side might be called noise.

That apparent orderliness is not always an assurance of good complexity is illustrated by bureaucracy; for, hidden beneath its facade of orderliness is arbitrary rule making, producing a maze and clutter of rules that seem to come from nowhere, that suddenly one must deal with and learn about (an all too familiar example being tax rules, through which no principle of common sense or equity will guide us, but we must refer line by line to a guidebook for each item).

The main point about the information of bad complexity is that it is a source of noise: useless as signal and confusing to what signals we make about the world. There is no elegant way to sum up bad complexity without giving directions that are about as complicated and uncertain as the situations they purport to explain. If reality is chaotic and noiselike, a symbol or map which truly represents that reality will probably itself be chaotic and noiselike. As news, philosophy, literature, and the arts accurately report a disorderly world, they, too, become noisy.

CHANNEL CLUTTER

Channel clutter, sometimes called chatter, occurs when too many parties (senders) try to use the same medium at the same time. Familiar examples are teenagers monopolizing the telephone or conversation when too many are talking at once. Chatter becomes noiselike when trivial messages crowd out important ones, or it is a strain to get a desired message among others.

Modern media invite people to talk more than they really need to. Telephoning, for example, has burgeoned to unprecedented levels; long distance is as chatty as local. Trivial calls add to the overload of networks at peak hours when it becomes impossible to get a long distance call through. Americans make four times as many phone calls as residents of any other country, using home attachments to give taped answers or put callers on hold while the receiver is on another line, according to a telephone company report in 1977.

Another example of channel clutter is the fad of citizens band radio during the 1970s. An advertisement announced:

Now you can put on your CB "ears" and join the exciting world of Citizens Band radio. Just tune in on any of the CB channels and get right-off-the-air reports of traffic jams, weather conditions, best alternate routes and emergencies. Having your own CB "ears" can save you time, money and gas. And you'll get a kick out of listening to the Good Buddies as they joke and chatter about "18-wheelers," "pregnant roller skates," "Tijuana taxi" and the "bears." Needs no license to operate.

By 1973, the CB radio boom had created "the world's largest, chattiest party line" with an estimated 7 million users, whose "rag-chewing" and "hamming" crowded all frequencies and generated continuous interference to established users. Not only that but people complained of unwanted CB conversations heard on telephones, even coming through their church sound system. Professionals complained of channels crowded with chatter. Also, by 1979, 9 million television viewers suffered some sort of interference from CB radios operating in their neighborhoods, according to estimate of the Federal Communications Commission.

Television talk shows also encourage chatter in that channel. Interviewers dig for something to talk about; an actress says, "I like yogurt with my bananas because it helps my complexion." The public listens, fascinated, taking in oceans of trivia for fear of missing one tidbit of sensation.

In the medium of paper and print, memo writing and paperwork have cluttered the channels of many organizations. No small factor is growing technical ease and speed of copying, word processing, and publishing. Publications can be turned out overnight, topical books printed within a few weeks after a news event, non-books compiled by clipping and splicing. Vanity presses urge new authors to publish. More and more people feel they have something to say publicly. Soon, it seems, everybody—dancers, penitentiary inmates, boxers—start to publish their books.

Of course, no one is in a position to say with authority that someone else's message is not important. But, plainly, chatter adds its part to a huge amount of public communication that, however interesting it is to senders, is trivial and boring to everyone else. When there is too much chatter, attention becomes shallow, one does not listen with whole-hearted interest but skims and scans restlessly, looking for something significant: high mobility, heavy appointments, many messages, many distractions, shallow engagement—busy boredom.

DEARTH OF FEEDBACK

A sixth way in which information becomes noiselike in modern society is lack of feedback while the volume of communication increases. Today media bombard; they do not answer us, so that messages seem random and chaotic from the receiver's point of view. Such abundance of information without feedback does not help solve problems but adds to the difficulty of finding the fact or meaning one wants. Beer (1972:31–32) observes that corporate managers are "engulfed in a sea of useless facts" very little of which is feedback to anything they have done or decided. In our information-loaded society, honest, constructive feedback is an exceedingly rare commodity, and it is hard to find any profession or institution, even family or community—even psychiatry—that has enough of it.

What does it mean to lack feedback? Lacking news of where one succeeded or failed puts a person in the predicament of the king who wore no clothes, unable to see what is wrong and rectify performance. How lack of feedback produces self-blindness would be quickly apparent to anyone who tried to cut his own hair without a mirror.

Even though polling is of some help, institutions usually receive too little feedback from evaluation of their practices and policies. Many public agencies and businesses try to look good in reports and shun real evaluations of their performances. To look at an annual report, you would never know that a business was poorly run. Most keep negative feedback a secret or avoid it altogether. A case in point is surgery and hospitals. According to Dr. George Crile, Jr., former head of surgery at Cleveland Clinic, the fee system of paying a surgeon for each surgery performed is wrong, and so is the secrecy regarding surgical outcomes. He advocates that surgeons be put on salary and hospitals be required to publish their death rates by surgical procedures. According to Dr. Crile, if every hospital had to list every type of surgery performed within its walls, along with the death rate for that procedure at that hospital, patients could shop for the hospital with the best success (Associated Press, April 4, 1979).

Small groups tend to avoid negative feedback by exerting pressure on their members toward conformity—commonly called "group think" (Janis, 1972). Members not wishing to seem disloyal withhold criticism of what the group is doing, fostering blind spots and self-righteous illusions.

Generally, persons receive too little feedback. Artists have been known to lurk anonymously about galleries where their works are shown, hoping to overhear candid comment. Face-to-face, the polite comment is "interesting" (hiding judgments that might range from good to terrible). In moral judgments, too, we are often reluctant to set people straight, but prefer to mind our own business and let them stew in their own juice.

However, dearth of feedback exacts its price. In a society poor in feedback, people are not paid enough attention. Identity problems abound, one expression of which is ego-screaming, the plea "look at me!" as people try to draw attention to themselves (Klapp, 1969:80–84).

The shortage of feedback is evident in performing arts, where there are simply not enough audiences to watch, hear, and appreciate all who would like to perform. This is especially evident in music, not only in student recitals but thousands of trained musicians who never get a chance to display their art—even if offered free. Recordings and a few stars take up almost all the attention. Likewise, there are for would-be authors, trained in journalism or writing courses, for whose output there are not enough readers. Performers line up in the wings waiting to be seen and heard, but no cue calls them on stage—voices have multiplied but not ears.

The upshot is that, in the midst of a deluge of communication without enough feedback, information becomes less interesting and more noise-like—more boring.

STYLISTIC NOISE

We live in an era of clashing life-styles and tastes, in which more communication has made people more aware of differences. People thrust their tastes upon one another. Music grates on the ears as "New Wave" challenges "rock" (Lull, 1982:128), "straight," "country," folk, and jazz. Cocaine snorters shock whiskey drinkers. The 1960s brought an explosion of styles—hippie, long-hair, psychedelic, unisex, Gay Lib, swinging, and black—rebelling against the established culture—just as, decades before, the 1920s brought bathtub gin, flaming youth, companionate marriage; and bobbed hair, short skirts and cigarettes for women (Allen, 1931).

Stylistic noise comes not from mere change of styles but clash of incompatible values, as when modernizing countries complain of "immoral" Western films or Anglo-American dominance of their media threatening their cultural identities. Stylistic noise always threatens some identity—presenting signals and models (noise) incompatible with the identity a person or group wishes to preserve. It not only fails to reinforce but blurs that identity. Such a threat might come from a signal grossly out of tune with an occasion—something so seemingly trivial as arriving inappropriately dressed, say in a T-shirt, at a formal party, thereby spoiling its tone, whether by offending the host or implying that dress standards need not be upheld. Basically, it is a matter of compatibility: people who like the same sounds can be loud together; those who have the same tastes can do as they please together. But even tight sectarian groups, such as the Amish, cannot altogether avoid stylistic noise. Today, television is bringing stylistic noise into indigenous cultures the world over (Granzberg, 1982; Katz, 1977). A pluralistic society with open boundaries runs into bewildering problems of stylistic noise, including loss of control over youth, who are much affected by what I call modeling noise (Klapp, 1978:96–98) from media, an array of dubious models—violent, lawless, and so on—which give little or no reinforcement to kinds of character parents wish to emphasize and blur and confuse values upheld by the schools.

Opening its media to almost any sort of message, a pluralistic society receives also a great deal of noise that looks like information but isn't.

PSEUDO-INFORMATION

I suspect that no one knows how much of the supply of public communication is pseudo-information, which purports to tell something but in fact tells nothing. Names such as hype, hokum, rhetoric, B.S., ballyhoo, shuck, schmalze, fake factor, buildup, puffery, and image building warn us not to take at face value much of what we hear even though one cannot pin down exactly what is wrong with it. This applies to statements in any medium that denote or connote something they do not deliver, as do many advertisements, certificates, warranties, diplomas, badges, and so on. Language often proliferates into pseudo-information as bafflegab, jargon, vogue words, or reifications that add no thought and stand in the way of clear thinking and communication.

Advertising does much to create pseudo-information by claiming differences among brands—gasolines, beers, cigarettes, automobiles, that are different in image or label but hardly anyone can distinguish in tests or performance (Key, 1973:83). A bewildering variety of drugs masquerade under fancy labels at higher prices. New brand names multiply pseudo-distinctions among products as market managers stretch their minds to invent product names, over 20,000 being registered annually by the U.S. Patent Office (*Saturday Review*, June 13, 1970, p. 60). Testimonials and images create an aura of prestige or desirability for one product that in fact is no different from others.

Likewise, public relations adds hype (hokum) to shows, sports events, pseudo-events (Boorstin, 1962), entertainers, and political personalities who need a style or image that is better than what they really are to get elected. Good performance isn't enough.

Pseudo-information comes also from fashions whose glittering novelty quickly turns to bad redundancy, as noted in Chapter 5. Here the pseudo-information consists of over-valuing the new and devaluing the old—distinctions that momentarily seem important but soon lose all importance, like messages written in disappearing ink.

Pseudo-information—purporting to say something—not only fails to inform but *mis*informs, puts one wrong, adds the burden of discounting, clearing up, and retracing steps, to whatever work was wasted in decoding. It ranges from zero information, which gets one nowhere, to negative information, which sets one back, defined by Harary and Batell (1978) as that which causes the receiver to deviate from the optimal decision path in reaching his goal, that is, to have to make more decisions than the minimum required for correct solution, such difference in bits measuring the amount of negative information. Another formulation is that of Watzlawick (1976:xiv), who distinguishes "disinformation" ("such knots, impasses and delusions as may come about in the voluntary process of actively seeking or of deliberately withholding information") from mere confusion ("breakdowns of communication and attendant distortions that arise involuntarily"). So pseudo-information—or disinformation or negative information—goes beyond mere mistakes and confusion to delusion requiring work to clear the mind of wrong decisions before one can make right ones. It has an ensnaring character, requiring one to disentangle oneself, retrace wrong decisions and turnings, before reaching the right path. So pseudo-information makes the world seem fuller of different things than it actually is, and considerably more costly.

Although its value is zero or negative, pseudo-information takes just as much work to process as does real information. In that respect it is like counterfeit money (acting as noise to real money). Like counterfeit, pseudo-information makes one feel richer so long as it passes and buys what it claims to be worth. Coming in the same kind of package as the real, it may circulate for a time and some may never be found out. But, ultimately, one loses from it, if only in ways such as embarrassment, disillusionment, and loss of good faith.

When so many enjoy being fooled, it is hardly necessary to suppose that malefactors such as con men are behind all pseudo-information. But, in a broader sense, perhaps the largest source is manipulation, the tactic of getting someone to do something without letting him in on the secret. Contemporary literature has made the public painfully aware of how much manipulation is going on—books and articles with titles like *Seeing Through Shuck* (Kostelanetz, 1972); "The Fake Factor" (Herzog, 1973); *Man the Manipulator* (Shostrum, 1967); *I Can Sell You Anything* (Wrighter, 1972), offering to "spill the beans" about weasel words, deceptive claims, visual gimmicks, emotion-charged symbols, and psychological tricks used by Madison Avenue advertisers as described by Herbert Schiller in *The Mind Managers* (1973); *Subliminal Seduction* (Key, 1973), and *The Manipulators* (Sobel, 1976). Crusades to protect consumers and voters are mounted by groups such as Common Cause and the Nader organization. The Federal Trade Commission tries to restrain phony testimonials and endorsements in TV commercials. Admired entertainers freely admit trying to "con" their audiences. John Lennon of the Beatles said:

We know we're conning them, because we know people want to be conned. Let's stick that in there, we say. That'll start them puzzling. I bet Picasso sticks things in. I bet he's been laughing about it for the last eighty years. Beethoven is a con, just like we are now. He was just knocking out a bit of work, that was all (quoted by Hunter Davies, 1968:82).

We all know that elections have become an image-building, promotional operation in which candidates are sold in much the same way as are products. Even "selling the Deity" is "big business" (Fiske, 1972). All seems to be con. It is hard to find a public message that has not been rigged or jiggled by somebody.

Manipulation withholds information to achieve a strategy not possible with full disclosure. If the total information of a frank message is H, then what gets through after a manipulator withholds the purpose, meaning, and facts (M) is $H-M$. So manipulation acts like noise degrading information of messages, thereby increasing the receiver's entropy. Manipulation makes people unable to reach their own goals—the world becomes strangely thwarting; one cannot steer his ship but finds himself arriving where he had not intended to go, almost as though there were another hand at the tiller. However, enough manipulation is perceived so that polls show trust in leaders and institutions is low, and people are in the habit of discounting messages without knowing which is counterfeit—a condition oddly like inflation. So manipulation builds a world that will probably fail sooner or later.

But, when pseudo-information is so easy to generate and unchallenged, could it build a whole empire of falsehood like the Nazi Third Reich with its folk and race mythology and tragic costs? Orwell's *1984* shows us a fictional society mesmerized and unable to withdraw from pseudo-information. This raises the question of false consciousness: whether a culture could be so loaded with pseudo-information and ensnared by placebos (Chapter 10) that it becomes like a hall of distorting mirrors in which one could not tell which image was accurate. If the view through the picture tube becomes reality, how does one test that reality?

SHEER OVERLOAD

Finally, information becomes noiselike, however good or bad it may be, by its sheer volume or rate exceeding channel capacity.

We are aware of the burden of handling ever larger amounts of information. Individuals vary in their capacities; but at today's levels of communication, with every bridge groaning and creaking under the traffic, it would be hard to find anyone fairly well educated and broadly concerned who was not in some way or at some time suffering from information overload. However hard they try, people are more and more swamped by communication; they can give attention to less and less of the total. Every year thousands of pages of books, reports, and theses stack up in libraries without being read. Narrowing attention is most conspicuous regarding technical publications; for example, a survey showed that the average number of readers of any single paper in the *Journal of the American Chemistry Society* was four (Rapoport, 1976). Abstracts and computer data pools are not all that much help; a doctor complained, "Even from the computer I get thirty pages of printout about one disease when I have time to read only two." The mountain of reportage begins to look like a comic scene of a broker entangled in ticker tape: will we finally be buried in an avalanche of print that there is no time to read? On the audio-visual side, television viewing seems to have reached a limit: 1979 was the first year of no growth in watching beyond six and one-half hours daily. Through all media a flood of information is overwhelming human channel capacity. And in this capacity, the most crucial bottleneck is coding, excessive difficulty of which has already been mentioned as a source of noise.

A large amount and high rate of information act like noise when they reach overload: a rate too high for the receiver to process efficiently without distraction, stress, increasing errors, and other costs making information poorer. If the human channel capacity for a given task—say supermarket checker—is eight bits per second, but the checker is trying to handle ten bits, then perhaps it is reasonable to say that two bits are acting like noise, interfering with information, increasing errors and omissions, and so on. In such cases, one might say, information gets in its own way.

The notion of channel capacity is necessary in order to say how communication could have a bottleneck. It is like a pipe diameter limiting the rate of water flow. All components through which communication flows, living or not, are regarded as channels, each with its own capacity. Channel capacities have been determined for such things as cells, crustaceans, nerves of a cat, the retina, endocrine glands, and entire higher organisms; for example, at a nerve synapse the highest theoretical rate of information transmission has been calculated to be in the range of 1,000 to 3,000 bits per second (MacKay and McCulloch, 1952). Different media (violin versus piano, radio versus television, wires versus optical fibers) have their own channel capacities; as do persons for different communication functions (musical performance, speedwriting, lecturing, Morse decoding, aircraft recognition). For impromptu speaking, Quastler and Wulff (1955) found that the maximum transduction rate was about 26 bits per second, with a mean rate of about 18, whereas oral reading reached about 35 bits. John P. van Gigh (1976) compared various jobs as to the information processing load on workers' channel capacity, defined as "the maximum information processing rate or maximum entropy in bits/unit of time which can be handled through it." The maximum information processing rate in industrial jobs was estimated to be about 8.0 bits/second, most jobs being below this load, but certain ones, such as manual supermarket checking, taxing the channel capacity of workers. A message might go through a variety of channels—from a human mind through a telephone wire to another mind, which puts it into talk of a committee, which then transforms it into a recommendation that goes to an executive, whose order via a xeroxed letter goes to others, who issue a press release, and so on. At the simplest level, channel capacity is a matter of transmission, that is, measuring an output performance or message transduced against the signal input (the output message from a channel always being less discriminable than the input because of a certain amount of noise inherent in the channel). The trouble, then, is not in how much or what kinds of information come at us but varying limits of channels. Physical conductors and systems easily outstrip humans; for example, the channel capacity of industrial workers is about eight bits per second (Van Gigh, 1976), whereas physical conductors and computers can easily surpass this (for example, laser via optical fibers can now carry 1,400 simultaneous conversations, and may ultimately reach 1 billion bits per second). So the weakest link in a vast chain of communication is often the human brain, because, for all its powers of abstraction, it is severely limited in channel capacity.

Some of the limitation is in perceptual discrimination. Experiments by George A. Miller (1967:8, 18–25, 48) showed that humans have difficulty making discriminative judgments of sound, color, taste, and so on when alternatives go beyond the "magic number seven." "There seems to be some limitation built into us either by learning or by the design of our nervous systems" which limits what we can perceive immediately without help from some device such as counting.

We are able to perceive up to about six dots (marbles, beans, dice marks, musical tones) accurately without counting; beyond this errors become frequent. . . . This ceiling is always very low. Indeed, it is an act of charity to call a man a channel at all. Compared to a telephone or television channels, a man is better characterized as a bottleneck (Miller, 1967:8, 18–25, 48).

It does not help to add more hardware if the bottleneck is in the software.

Neuropsychologists have thrown new light on our mental capacities by observing that the left and right sides of the brain have different functions and channel capacities (Buchsbaum, 1979; Budzinski, 1977; Ferguson, 1980). The left side seems to be better with words, mathematics, calculation, criticism, analysis, goal-directed work, and literal thinking; the right is better with melody, pattern, qualities, intuition, meditation, metaphor, and nonverbal (body) language and art. The left brain responds more quickly to the right side of the visual field than vice versa; and, perhaps just because of its promptness, is often overloaded with inappropriate information it is not best fitted to handle—another bottleneck. The left brain is more vulnerable and overloads sooner because its optimal number of categories into which to sort information is lower than that of the right brain. Experiments showed

the right hemisphere to be superior when the number of categories or elements to be distinguished was large, five or seven. Two other studies found that the left hemisphere is superior when the number of categories or elements to be distinguished is small, about two (Pendse, 1978:426).

Some suspect that problems such as alcoholism and schizophrenia may be due to left brain channel overload while right brain signals are neglected—perhaps a bias of Western culture, which overloads the left hemisphere with calculative, verbal, digital information while inadvertently neglecting pattern recognition and intuition by the right. If there are such differences of hemispheric function, then much information is bound to seem noiselike when unsuited to the hemisphere trying to process it. What it adds up to is that some of our information overload comes from trying to do a job with the wrong hemisphere, or the noisy business of one side drowning out signals from the other. The remedy seems to be either achieving brain wave coherence or making less noise on one side interfering with signals of the other.

Though the brain is a weak link, it does not follow that many heads are necessarily better than one in overcoming information overload. J.G. Miller (1960) found that teams of four had lower channel capacities than individuals at the same task. In these experiments four people were required to cooperate in coordinating information that appeared on a screen. The performance of two teams leveled off at about three bits of input per second, showing the point at which overload occurred. The channel capacity was found to be between 2 and 2.5 bits of output per second. When overload occurred, certain kinds of behaviors became frequent: (1) omitting information from the process, (2) processing erroneous information, (3) queuing—holding off some responses during rush periods with the hope that it may be possible to catch up during a lull, (4) filtering—selecting some kinds of information and leaving others, (5) cutting categories—discriminating with less precision (for example, instead of saying "I see yellow," saying, "I see a light color" or "I see a color"), (6) using multiple channels, as in decentralization; and (7) escaping from the task.

It seems reasonable that if networks multiply the amount and kinds of communication, they could also multiply noise and difficulties with channel limits, physical and human, no small example of which is the troubles of bureaucracy. In small groups, various network patterns have been found to have different channel capacities; for example, a "wheel" or mesh has a better capacity than a "chain" because several lines can carry a distributed load (for example, a committee dividing up an assignment), but studies also show that strain increases on the central position in a "wheel" when information increases, as measured by increased time to perform tasks, reaching a "saturation" point that exceeds the ability of the individual to process information (Gilchrist, 1955). So, a wheellike organization gains in efficiency by sending all its messages to one executive, but at some point it loses efficiency when the executive suffers overload. Larger organizations have more channels, types of networks, and resources, so presumably can handle bigger loads; though it is possible for them to have difficulties of individuals and small groups compounded. Meier (1962, 1972) described policies adopted by organizations such as a library or stock exchange for coping with overloads of incoming requests including queuing, queuing priorities, destruction of lowest priorities, assembly-line processing of repeated requests, branch facilities, middlemen, mobile reserves, performance standards, search for the "magic formula," customer self-service, reducing standards of performance, escape, and working ritualistically to rule.

It comes down to this: whatever the group pattern, the frequency of overload and low channel capacity of humans come from the burden of coding, which, as I said, is the hinge of the door of communication— and also its most crucial bottleneck. Wherever complex judgment and creativity are required (as in recognizing aircraft patterns, tasting wine, interpreting languages, composing literature, directing an orchestra, judging an art show, performing a sport, even checking in a supermarket), higher faculties and both sides of the brain must be used to do coding, the complexity of which can be visualized by deciphering a cryptogram or trying to translate English into Egyptian hieroglyphics. Every information transfer requires decoding, encoding, and/or recoding; that we take such work for granted does not lessen it—at the human level reference to a huge stock of symbols or making new ones. As the stock of both symbols and raw information grows, people must spend more time sorting and relating new bits and deciding from what code, if any, they come and into which code they go. What it adds up to is a growing burden of coding from ever larger masses of information, much of which is unsorted and unconnected, like the unfitted pieces of a jigsaw puzzle. The higher the meaning, the more judgmental the task, the more pieces there are to fit into a more intricate pattern. So our society, for all its hardware, and however large its organizations, suffers information overload because the bottleneck of coding has not been widened. It is still just as hard to make complex judgments of pattern and meaning as ever—and more need to be made!

We have seen ways—loudness, decoding difficulty, disconnectedness, bad complexity, channel clutter, dearth of feedback, stylistic noise, pseudo-information, and sheer overload—in which information becomes noise-like and degrades communication. Because noise is essentially confusion in messages, the higher its proportion in the environment, the less we learn and the less meaning we get.

This helps us see why it is possible to be bored with increasing information, why communication can become boring in spite of much variety and entertainment. In a noisy environment of information, one receives little news that is of interest because it is relevant to a particular person or purpose. The environment can be a wasteland of uninteresting and unwelcome stimuli—to which banality adds its part—in which feedback is poor, so performance does not improve, and opportunities for self-expression are meagre. Crowded with people, where voices have multiplied but not ears, such an environment is mass society at its worst, with all the problems of identity and meaning one would expect.

Our thesis here is that it is not so much the sheer amount of information that is the problem but the fact that information becomes noiselike.

The next chapter portrays accumulation of information without proportionate meaning—a gap that grows ever wider as the speed of accumulation increases—due basically to the fact that meaning formation (tenuous at best in mass society) is slower than information accumulation, and especially so when information becomes noiselike.

8

THE SLOW HORSE

Events burst upon us with staggering rapidity. A dozen mind-boggling moral dilemmas might be presented in the evening news. What is the meaning of these events? We get a few minutes to ponder one question before the next comes on. Do these provisional decisions coalesce into well-grounded positions and ultimately character and wisdom? Or is it more likely that large questions remain unsettled, and we go on to new ones, dissatisfied with what we know, no wiser than before?

In the meanwhile, information floods on, demanding that something be done. Computers are rushed into operation to supply new data faster. But lack of data wasn't the problem before—why should it be now? Overload rather than scarcity seems a fit description of the supply of information, much of which, as we have pointed out, consists of bad redundancy and noise.

Facing such a flood, we find ourselves in the familiar, uneasy dilemma between restriction of information and skimming or scanning superficially, neither of which is entirely satisfactory. On one hand, we may close off information by avoidance, filtering, editing, or even boredom as a withdrawal of attention. A common way is by specialization of work within a narrow sphere of expertise or formal responsibility (as I recollect C. P. Snow said, "Scientists regard it as a major intellectual virtue to know what not to think about"). Another way people defend themselves from too much information is simply called prejudice or ideology. Hostile outbursts, scapegoating, backlashes, and repressive legislation may be closing reactions to the strain of information overload. Years ago Festinger (1957:3, 13) explained cognitive dissonance. When they are "psychologically uncomfortable," people will "try to reduce dissonance and achieve consonance." For example, they will "avoid situations and information which would likely increase the dissonance"; they will seek evidence to confirm decisions already made and avoid that which contradicts what they believe; if challenged, they will act homeostatically to preserve their own point of view, say by rationalization or by "selective exposure" to views which support their own position (Carter et al., 1969; Freedman and Sears, 1965). If they belong to a cult whose prophecies have failed, they will talk all the harder and optimistically to persuade people to join (Festinger, Riecken, and Schachter, 1956).

The other horn of the dilemma of how to cope with too much information is striving to cover it all by rapid scanning, giving superficial attention to things as they come up, not dwelling long (reading reviews and abstracts instead of books; passing up heavy for light thought, poetry for facts, long for short conversation, and so on). One cost of such rapid scanning is distraction, living in the front of one's mind, lacking time to connect deeply with one's inner self (or right brain, as some now put it). Hastily scanning, switching, and gulping gives people a sort of chronic indigestion of information in which bits do not assimilate into character and wisdom.

So each of these ways of coping with information overload carries an uncomfortable cost. One puts us into the predicament of the ostrich with its head in the sand, the other into "skating on thin ice." Neither gets us far in solving the meaning crisis of modern times. Both reflect our human channel limits in coping with the information flood. On the societal scale we observe lags of decision, consensus, and meaning, from differential rates of information processing throughout our society.

Even if people managed to keep up by reading or otherwise getting into their heads what is going on, they would sooner or later realize uncomfortably that all that information was not solving problems at a rate plausibly to be expected—that in advanced societies problems were proliferating along with information. Sociologists (Ogburn, 1922; Chapin, 1924, 1928; Hart, 1945) long ago noted that cultural lags, as they were called, resulted from material culture growing exponentially but hoped that with more knowledge and better prediction people could catch up. As time went on, one saw uncomfortably that lists of social problems were getting longer, new ones, such as pollution and drug abuse, along with old ones, such as mounting crime, mental ill health, and unemployment. There was a growing sense of poor coordination in the midst of communication, widening gaps between problems and solutions; it seemed the more we knew, the farther behind we got. By the 1970s, so many problems had erupted that the very idea of progress was thrown into crisis; advanced technology and piling up of social science information had little or no effect in hastening the solution of problems; there was a sense of futility; indeed, it almost seemed that for every step forward society was losing two. Such ineffectualness of social policy seems to show not merely that information is not being applied but that overload or clutter of information is part of the problem—that society is in the predicament illustrated by the committee that (actually) reported, "We started with two plans of action and now we have narrowed them down to eight."

Such ineffectualness comes from at least three sorts of lag beyond that of decoding, namely: of decision, consensus, and meaning formation. At close view, decision lag is illustrated by the executive battling with an in-basket load. (Some idea of what a modern executive faces comes from the fact that during the eight years that Dean Rusk was secretary of state 2,100,000 cables went out of the State Department with his signature—quite a load even if he merely signed them.) So also the housewife at her kitchen phone, or chauffering children, or holding a second job; the salesman on his calls, the student with his course schedule; the professional seeing clients and making reports; the entire "harried middle class" (Linder, 1970) may feel the in-basket filling too rapidly for good decisions, trying to fit more things than go into one career or style of life.

Even if individuals can decide promptly about their own in-baskets, lags in consensus come from inability to give up old views more quickly and come together with others in new ways; even communication of new messages is laborious; time is needed to persuade or, educate. One might have to build a political party to support policies no current one accepts.

Some idea of consensus lag comes from the incredible legislative burden faced by Congress. During the 1977–78 session, congressmen introduced 22,313 public and private bills and resolutions; the House filed reports on 1,810, the Senate, 1,413; they passed 3,211 bills and resolutions, with 804 bills finally enacted into law; and managed in two years to confirm 124,730 military and civilian nominations. A senator describes the burden: "We are losing control of what we are doing ... there isn't enough time in a day to keep abreast ... having to attend so many committee and subcommittee meetings, listening to the lobbyists, having to worry about problems of constituents, and, of course, keeping a close eye on politics back home." Congressmen flit in and out of hearings, a minute here, an hour there. One said, "I can't be everywhere at the same time. And I also have to race to the floor for quorum votes or votes on bills whenever that damned bell rings. It's insane" (Szulc, 1979:20, 22). In one view this could be taken as a tribute to speed of consensus formation, but in another it is a confession of superficiality and bad complexity (clutter)—not viable consensus—of legislative decisions.

Consensus lags continually at three levels in most public problems. First, science and scholarship fail to keep up, by theory building and research, with the flood of raw data from the environment, perhaps because of retrieval problems, overspecialization, lack of funding for research, or inability to develop unified theory that coordinates new information with old. Science and scholarship feed their already lagging output into a second level of decision making, government and administration, which have their own reasons, such as bureaucratic rigidities and political goals, for being out of touch with the scientific community, for failing to use theoretical information effectively even if it is available. Flooded by crises and popular pressures, operating largely without the benefit of scientific theory or even indicators, government and administration are slow and inept in developing policies, and by piecemeal or repressive measures may actually make problems worse, feeding back into the mounting crises. Below these two decision levels is a third level, public opinion, which exerts some effective pressure on government and administration but is on the whole apathetic and uninformed, tends to avoid cross pressures, and is hard to mobilize—yet sometimes rises to veto group action (for example, paralysis of policy by vocal minorities who lack the power to get what they want but have enough leverage to block experts or even a majority decision). A case in point is, perhaps, the fate of water fluoridation measures in American community politics. When fluoridation was put into effect quietly, there was no trouble; but when put to a referendum, angry opposition, even paranoid elements, often defeated the proposals (Crain, Katz, and Rosenthal, 1969). Such cases illustrate sources of lag that seem to be built into the formation of democratic consensus.

A great deal of lag in decision and consensus is due to homeostatic need to preserve redundancy, which operates at all levels of living systems. That is, even if technical information is available for solving a problem (for example, a plan for efficient mass transportation to reduce use of automobiles), and the communication time required to clear or make channels, diffuse information, and educate the public is not long, there will still be homeostatic resistance from individuals and groups who want to preserve their own ways of doing things, defend their own structures, and persevere in their own goals. So one saw resistance to the change in habits required by the energy crisis, such as car pooling, waiting for gasoline, using mass transit, not driving on long vacation trips, turning down the thermostat, and wearing more clothing indoors. Habits are the essence of individual self-conserving patterns. Similarly, groups tend to preserve themselves. Suppose a group of medical doctors were efficiently informed of a better type of treatment. However good the communication has been, we should still expect them to be slow to adopt it if it requires radical change in the structure of practice—for example, some form of socialized medicine, or giving more relative status to nurses, paramedics, and technicians. "Keep things the way we like it" is the whole thrust of homeostasis. No different would we expect the response of other groups to be, such as labor unions, teachers' associations, churches, even radical political parties, if their own structures were threatened by information. Even scientists as a collectivity act homeostatically, if we may so judge intolerance toward experiments like those of J.B. Rhine on ESP, or toward theories like those of Immanuel Velikovsky (to which controversy a special issue of *The American Behavioral Scientist* under editorship of Alfred de Grazia was devoted in 1963).

There is an even slower horse in the race with change. Behind immediate decision and consensus comes the meaning of it all. Meaning has a reputation for arriving late—indeed, the highest meaning, wisdom, is also slowest to arrive. Beckett has his characters "waiting for Godot," leaving the audience in doubt as to whether Godot will arrive. If each new bit of information were like a "yes" or "no" answer in a 20 questions game, life might have the excitement of following the clues of a detective story. But bits don't add up, each new fact is unrelated to the preceding. We can see this in education. As a university teacher, I can say after 25 years of experience, that the average instructor teaches as much as he can of his own subject without the faintest idea of how it all adds up in the student's mind with the other subjects he is taking. Nor is there any testimony from most graduates that they have reduced the meaning gap when they finally put on their cap and gown. On the contrary, they enter careers realizing that changes have made nonsense of institutional values such as the idea that all must work (in a looming age of cybernation and guaranteed incomes), or that economic growth is good. The conventional wisdom seems absurd, but the new wisdom is yet to be found.

A meaning gap is not merely inability to come to a decision or policy, but failure to agree on what a policy should be for. For example, a group of engineers might have plenty of expertise to build a bridge, yet might be doubting where to build the bridge, whether to build it at all, or even whether to be engineers, or whether to have a technocratic society. For the latter two kinds of question, their calculations are of no help. So I would define a *meaning gap* as an inability of people in the same society to agree on larger patterns, purposes, and values even when they share the same factual information, which is piling up at a rate faster than they can agree about purposes and values, and may lead to a sense of absurdity. Such a paradox flouts what we normally expect of information: that it should bring people together, make sense of the world, and finally hand us the crown of wisdom on a golden platter of happiness. No such thing!

One way to conceive the slowness in making sense is by the following metaphor. Suppose one is seated at a table fitting pieces of a gigantic jigsaw puzzle. From a funnel overhead, pieces are pouring onto the table faster than one can fit them. Most of the pieces do not match—indeed they do not all belong to the same puzzle. In this metaphor, the pieces of the puzzle represent facts rapidly accumulating; the pattern is the meaning, slowly emerging, perhaps never found. The irregularity and confusion in the heap of pieces, impeding finding a fit, might be called the noise of the puzzle. Suppose the puzzle you are trying to fit together is the pattern, the very meaning, of your life. Then too many bits pouring in faster than one can make sense of them would mean being endlessly suspended in judgment and restricted to superficial facts, unable to develop a coherent and profound life philosophy. The different colors and textures of the pieces of the jigsaw puzzle refer to the fact that not only does the information not refer to the same topic (especially ourselves) but it consists of different kinds of information—say poetry and statistics or mysticism and logic—that don't fit together by any kind of reckoning.

What I suggest is that the lag from which society suffers be expressed as a relationship between different sorts of information: on the one hand, mere information conceived as reduction of uncertainty in any binary (yes-or-no) choice, commonly measured in bits; and, on the other, mean-

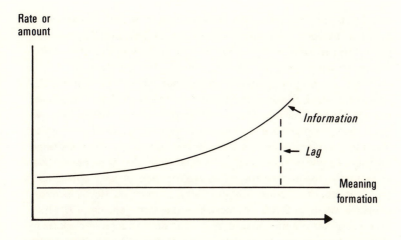

Figure 8.1
Lag of Meaning Formation Behind Information Accumulation

ing as information about the relation of something to a pattern or scheme of which one is part—an awareness that is necessarily subjective. Mere information that is additive, digital, or analytical, accumulates easily by being counted or categorized; whereas meaning, being subjective, and referring to synthetic or holistic properties that cannot be reduced to the sum of parts, might be called a higher sort of information that does not come easily, let alone inevitably, from a growing heap of mere information. In a race between these two sorts of information, we expect information processing, for the sake of practical decision and working consensus, to be a fast horse, whereas meaning is a slow horse—and the highest meaning, wisdom, is last of all to arrive, if ever.

This race between a fast horse called mere information and a slow horse called meaning, leaping hurdles of noise, is diagrammed in Figure 8.1 showing the hypothetical lag. This diagram is meant to indicate that mere information, however measured, grows rapidly—even exponentially—in modern society; whereas meaning formation, by whatever indicators or measures, is expected to be fairly steady or level, so declining proportionally to information and noise. The reason for the fairly level curve of meaning formation is that society is already using most of its channel capacity for coding and decoding symbols and for synthesizing new meaning; and has invented no new ways; while raw information pours in faster than ever, from sources such as science, technological invention, modernization, and changing fashion (represented by the rising curve). So the paradox is possible (at least in some ranges of the information growth curve): the more knowledge, the less meaning.

Why is meaning formation so slow compared with growth of sheer information? One reason seems to be simply technological. The channel, storage, and retrieval capacities of electronic hardware are rapidly growing. Striking examples are increases of channel capacities of laser optical fibers and of microcomputers. In electronic communication, the channel capacity of a line or wave is called its bandwidth, that of an optical fiber being vastly greater than that of an electric wire. A laser optical fiber the thickness of a human hair can carry as much as 10,000 ordinary telephone wires, or 8,000 TV channels, at one time (Jennings, 1979:106). Microcomputer systems can be used by half a dozen people all performing different tasks at the same time. Most of this is technological gain, whereas corresponding human capacities, though improvable by learning, are much more limited. Better information processing—computing, storage, retrieval, scanning—can speed the flow and exchange of data but is of little help in reading the printout, deciding what to do about it, agreeing with others, or finding higher meaning. This is not to say that conferencing (video, audio, computer) will not help (see Hiltz and Turoff, 1978; Simmons, 1979). But sooner or later it comes down to the human bottleneck—the channel limits of Socrates.

A second reason for lag in meaning is that its formation requires thought, pondering, wondering—even dreaming—all time-consuming things that only humans do. Pondering, distinguished from calculative thinking (Heidegger, 1966), is inherently slow, as suggested by synonyms like brooding, contemplating, meditating, deliberating, mulling things over. The pace of modern life, with media messages urgent, strident, and shifting, allow little time for pondering before new items demand attention. Exegesis, hermeneutics, legal interpretation, and scientific theorizing all take time. To be sure, revelations, intuitions, breakthroughs, and religious conversions do occur suddenly but seldom—perhaps once in a lifetime.

Talk has always been a major process of meaning formation whatever its form—discussion, debate, brainstorming, counseling, psychotherapy, encountering, group therapy, chat, gossip, rumor (Shibutani, 1966; Rosnow and Fine, 1976). But, here again, slowness characterizes most talk compared with mere information transmission, if only because it is dial-ogical and waits for the other's thought and answer. Deep discussion, epitomized by Socrates' teaching, takes hours, even years or decades, to reach meaning other than superficial. (Modern higher education, with lecture the predominant mode of instruction, and complaints about cram-ming and regurgitating, seems to illustrate such superficiality of meaning.) Even with the help of audio-visual, computer and video-conferencing technology, there is little reason to believe that meaning formation by pondering and talk has speeded up since the time of Socrates—we still use the same old slow ways.

Of course, people do turn to authorities (commentators, pundits, judges, experts, oracles, diviners, opinion leaders) for quick answers. But this often produces a welter of opinions, with little consensus and less trust, that seldom speak for more than a minority—the very multipli-cation of authoritative claims (health food fads, for example) adding ironically to the bulk of information needing interpretation. So—even helped by interpretations of opinion leaders and the enormous speed of information diffusion—we see not gain in meaning but a growing mountain of information about which people do not know what to think.

Ritual, ceremony, and drama are major ways of bestowing and pre-serving the meaning of events and persons—part of "good" redundancy. Modern society has lots of ritual, if one includes such things as political inaugurations, party conventions, parades, military exercises, sports spec-tacles, television quiz games, and serial dramas viewed faithfully by large followings. But it can be argued that much of that ritual and quasi-ritual is poor or banal, and fails to bestow much meaning and identity upon participants, a case being the impersonality of mass college graduations (Klapp, 1969). Let us note that many "conversions" by mass evangelists like Billy Graham are found to be temporary (Johnson, 1971).

A central component of ritual is vicarious experience, from which people draw meaning through a sort of emotional hitchhiking on the affairs of others, real or fictional—something we all do, but for which film and television enormously amplify opportunities. Celebrities and popular heroes today provide myths, identification with which adds rom-ance to lives otherwise possibly drab. But we cannot count this as a simple gain in meaning if it occurs among people whose real-life rela-tionships are shallow or anomic as is common in mass society or if it is banal. In that case, vicarious experience is a substitute—a lower grade of meaning—at least not equivalent to meaning from real people in social networks; therefore unable to fill the place of what it compensates for completely, though offsetting the meaning gap somewhat.

Much of the trouble centers on the fact that, unlike information, which can be generated and multiplied almost mechanically, meanings seem to require natural processes of indigenous communication networks, including the slow growth of languages, beliefs, traditions, "we" feeling, and connections of status—all of which might be called "roots." Such indigenous nets support the individual, help him to realize his own meaning through feedbacks that are complex and may require time to complete (even ancestral debts), and help him to understand his world through gatekeepers and opinion leaders. It should be noted that there are two essential cycles of feedback necessary for meaning. One is input of discursive information, the basis of decisions, theories, techniques, and practical adaptations. The other essential cycle is of nondiscursive feedback, through roles, emotional gestures, ritual, and silent signals such as body language, which tells how others feel about us, how we feel about ourselves, and supports social feelings such as sympathy, friendliness, trust, sincerity, and tact, on which role-playing depends. Such feedback charges the batteries of social sentiment and makes people feel alive to one another. Without enough of it, people feel a sense of emotional shallowness and emptiness. Yet it is quite possible to communicate overloads of irrelevant facts, news, and such discursive information, while neglecting or losing the nondiscursive signals of social feeling and concern. Meanings hinge not on single information decisions but on a complex process of interactive support that always takes longer—maybe a lifetime.

When we do look at social networks in urban society, we find them typically sparse and diffuse—lots of acquaintances who do not know one another, widely spread, quickly moving—surely not the rich, dense worlds of gossip one finds in certain small communities (Blumenthal, 1932; Mitchell, 1969; Christian, 1972), where people draw much meaning from daily interaction with neighbors. The main point seems to be that urban mobility erodes the infrastructure from which meaning grows—the fabric of friendship, reciprocity, sense of place, roots. Mass media take the place of such infrastructure, though not sufficiently, as I have noted.

For such reasons—speed of technological processing of information, slowness of pondering and talk, the welter of authorities, poverty of ritual, vicarious compensation, weakness of networks, and mobility eroding the infrastructure—we expect meaning formation to be slow or insufficient compared with the speed and amount of information accumulating in modern society. So society suffers a growing gap between input of factual information and the construction of meanings, especially shared values, "we" feeling, and a sense of togetherness—unable to construct meanings fast enough to give its members a sense of living in a common world in which they can believe.

Perhaps meaning lag as we have described it can be boiled down to the following points: (1) rapid accumulation and diffusion of information beyond the human capacity to process it, and (2) inability of meaning, the slow horse, to keep up, due to (a) increase in noiselike characteristics of information making it harder to extract meaning: loudness, decoding difficulty, disconnectedness, bad complexity, channel clutter, dearth of feedback, stylistic noise, pseudo-information, and sheer overload—in such ways, one might say, information gets in its own way; and (b) slowness or insufficiency of meaning-forming processes: pondering and talk, the welter of authorities, poverty of ritual, vicarious compensation, weakness of networks, and mobility eroding the infrastructure of meaning.

As an information society develops such noisy and meaning-hindering characteristics, we have some explanation of why its communication becomes boring in spite of a high level of variety and entertainment, the fundamental reason being that it is hard to extract meaning. In any case, boredom comes from recognizing—in a noisy situation or communication—a small chance of hearing anything really interesting. So the vast mountain of information today in a strange way becomes a measure of our meaninglessness.

Of course, to test such hypotheses empirically requires appropriately measuring and comparing rates and kinds of meaning formation with rates of other sorts of information processing, and of noise production. There are measures of meaning (such as the Osgood semantic differential) and of lack of meaning (such as scales of alienation and anomie), but there is little reason to doubt that more suitable methods can be developed to measure levels and parameters of meaning. Above all, meaning lag calls for study of how to speed meaning formation and how noise interferes with meaning. The full spectrum of social noise—beyond auditory—needs to be explored before one can talk accurately about loss of meaning from increase in noise or to what extent information becomes noise like (for example, how "loud" is a style or color? how noisy are celebrities as role models?). The purpose here has been merely to distinguish some of the elements that need to be taken into account in a theory of noise and meaning lag in an information society.

Let us now look at a paradigm which likens information search to the tacking of a sailboat between variety and redundancy, which becomes boring if society veers too far either way. In this oscillation we seem to be in a dilemma between variety and redundancy, at both extremes of which lie boredom.

9

A METAPHORICAL MODEL

Having looked at banality and noise as ways in which information degrades, we need a theory that stresses the equal importance of variety and redundancy in the search for information and also its failure as signaled by boredom. I would like here to offer a paradigm—if only a metaphor—that can bring together many of the foregoing thoughts and facts about boredom. It uses four key concepts—information, entropy, redundancy, and variety. They come in pairs, as will be explained.

The first pair is information versus entropy. Information includes useful knowledge, learning, adaptation, potential, significant pattern, meaning, and wisdom. It is not merely the technical measure used in information theory. As MacKay (1969:56–57) explains, information as conventionally measured by communication engineers is not the same as information, message, or still less meaning as commonly understood, for example, by the semanticist:

> The trouble...appears to be due largely to a confusion of the concept of information with that of information-content—the confusion of a thing with a measure of a thing. Communication engineers have not developed a concept of information at all. They have developed a theory dealing explicitly with only one particular feature or aspect of messages "carrying" information—their unexpectedness or surprise value.... What Shannon and others did was to adapt and extend this method to the measurement of the unexpectedness of messages. Their measure of unexpectedness, the average logarithm of the improbability of the message...is not, therefore, *information* but simply a particular measure of what they termed *amount of information*.

Entropy is the negative of information and so is often used as a measure of it in communication. But in the physical world entropy is a tendency to confusion and randomness opposing information. A gain in information (negentropy) is a loss of entropy, and vice versa. Together, information and entropy comprise a continuum, providing a parameter that can be applied usefully to any life situation. In general, information means progress and entropy a step backward.

In this scheme, boredom can serve as an indicator of lack or loss of information (gain in entropy), that is, our sense that information is so poor that it does not arouse and merit interest, and that it is a waste of time to decode and process.

Another parameter comes from the other two key concepts, variety and redundancy, as also ways in which one can be bored. Suppose one wanted (for some unknown reason) to create a perfectly boring situation. According to this theory, there are two major possibilities. One would be a predicament of eternal sameness, suggestive of Beckett's "Waiting for Godot," or Sartre's "No Exit," or a psychologist's isolation chamber, where one was doomed to stay in an environment where one saw the same people, heard the same conversation, and saw and did the same things day after day. The other perfectly boring situation would be to require a person to remain forever where he was and to give continual attention to an enormous variety of changing items and bits of information that are quite insignificant—tell nothing he wants to know and add up to nothing by way of meaningful pattern. (This predicament was treated in the last chapter by the metaphor of an endless jigsaw puzzle, of which pieces are so diverse that they never fit together into a pattern.)

So in this view there are two ways of being bored. One is by redundancy, that is, too much information that is so similar that it tells little that is interesting and new. The other is by overload of variety so insignificant and noisy that it tells little of interest and does not fit into a meaningful pattern.

The theory implies that there are two states in which one can escape boredom. One is by variety so interesting and meaningful that it leads to discovery, learning, adaptation, invention, progress. The other is by redundancy so familiar, reliable, reassuring, supportive, communicative, and useful that it is prized and preserved and stirs warm memories— the purpose of ritual being to preserve such valuable redundancy.

Of the four states distinguished here (see Figure 9.1), the kind called "good" redundancy is most often unappreciated and even misunderstood. This is because people usually think of redundancy as functionless and superfluous as noted in Chapter 5. An important function of redundancy is to give a feeling of closeness to those who share it, for example

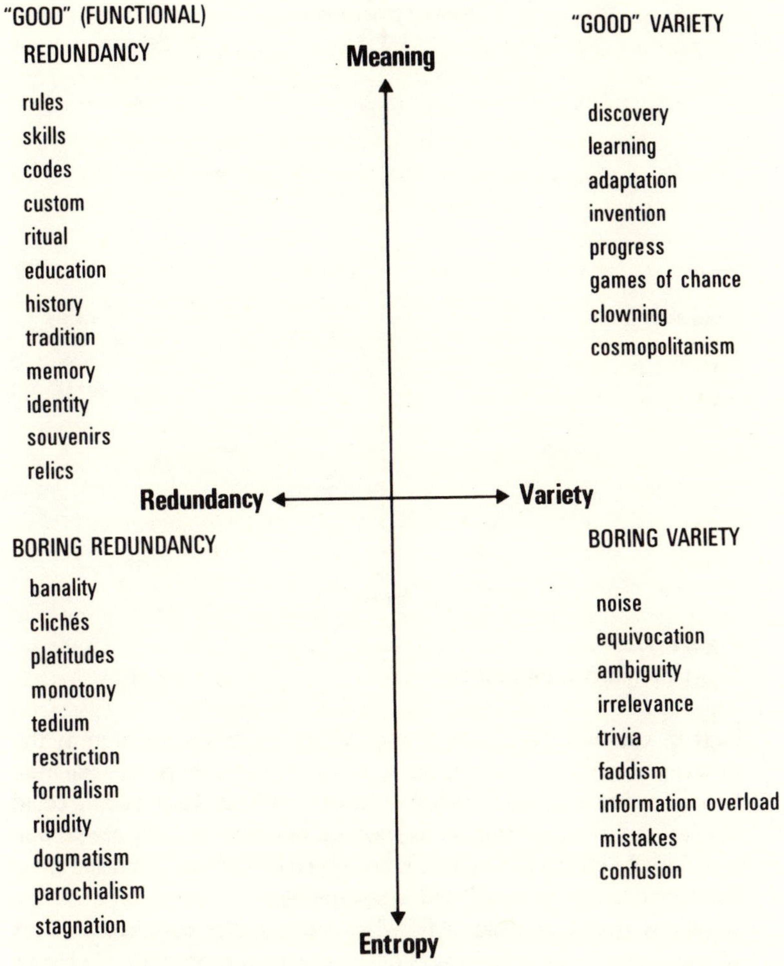

"GOOD" (FUNCTIONAL)
REDUNDANCY

"GOOD" VARIETY

Meaning ↑

rules
skills
codes
custom
ritual
education
history
tradition
memory
identity
souvenirs
relics

discovery
learning
adaptation
invention
progress
games of chance
clowning
cosmopolitanism

Redundancy ← → **Variety**

BORING REDUNDANCY

BORING VARIETY

banality
clichés
platitudes
monotony
tedium
restriction
formalism
rigidity
dogmatism
parochialism
stagnation

noise
equivocation
ambiguity
irrelevance
trivia
faddism
information overload
mistakes
confusion

Entropy ↓

Figure 9.1
Four Sectors of Information Search

ethnic costumes or religious symbols such as the crucifix or Hebrew cap (whereas "bad" redundancy is sterile uniformity without closeness, as from mass-produced clothing). Looking at its functions, one sees that redundancy is an exceedingly important component of social life—the

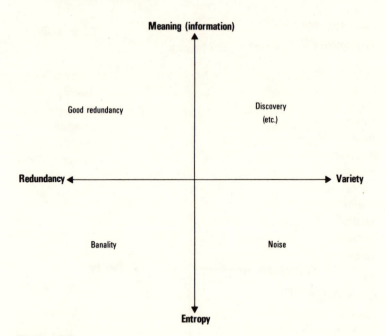

Figure 9.2
Chart of Information Search

basis of continuity as memory and culture; of communication as the
meaning of symbols; of resonance in relations with others (the common
band of redundancy, often called consensus, without which people could
not feel together); of identity as playback of memories telling who one
was. Such functional redundancy is preserved in tradition, rules and ritual
because it "earns its keep" and is not boring.

All this gives a fourfold table, which becomes for our theory a sort
of spatial chart. The four sectors of this chart are represented in Figure
9.2. For the sake of brevity I call the lower-left sector banality and the
lower-right noise. Everyone awake is in one of these quadrants, for the
simple reason that there is no place else to go.

Dynamically, there are two motive forces operating in this model.
One is the need for information and meaning. (I agree with Frankl
[1978:95] that human life is an unending search for meaning and that
boredom is a symptom of the "existential vacuum" of affluent society.)
The other is entropy working as a tendency toward disorder and mean-

inglessness. Entropy increases odds that one will drift into sectors of boring redundancy (banality) or boring variety (noise). Boredom is a signal that one has veered too far either way. (If a person catches himself yawning, he *discovers* that the information he is dealing with lacks enough meaning.) To escape from either extreme, one must move in the opposite direction, that is, from noise toward redundancy or from banality toward variety. The normal movement, then, is a continual oscillation, in which boredom—itself a motive—aids exploration to escape. For example, tired of travel, the adventurer returns home; tired of home, he travels; or tired of work, he plays; tired of play, he works.

We can visualize this interplay of meaning-search with entropy more clearly by the analogy of a ship sailing against the wind. One's maneuvering against entropy is like a ship tacking against the wind to get to its destination. The wind represents entropy which sailing must overcome, else the ship will be blown off course and perhaps never reach its destination. On Figure 9.3, the ship is conceived sailing north by tacking against a variable southerly wind. The ship cannot sail due north, because the wind is blowing south. It must, therefore, tack from eastward (variety) to westward (redundancy), and vice versa, trying to make its way toward its destination. But if the wind (representing entropy) is too strong, or the tacking is unskillful, the ship may fail to make headway, drift, or be driven too far to port or starboard, to more entropy, metaphorized by sandbars, reefs, being becalmed, distance from the destination, and so on. On the other hand, the ship may tack toward known waters and safe harbors (good redundancy), or venture into strange waters of discovery and exploration (good variety) while missing the shoals of redundancy and mistakes of bad variety.

According to our analogy, boredom is a sign of drifting into a losing sector, rather as a sounding indicates water too shallow, getting stuck in a boring predicament where one is aground or becalmed. It calls for a change of course or diversive exploration, which, by our paradigm, can be either back to familiar waters of good redundancy or into strange waters of discovery and creativity (good variety).

So by this metaphor, the normal movement of meaning-search is by continual change of course, toward redundancy for the sake of a sameness that is reassuring and reinforcing, and toward variety for the sake of adventure and discovery. A typical pattern of movement might be: seeking discovery (good variety)—drifting into confusion (bad variety)—falling back on the known (good redundancy)—feeling bored by restric-

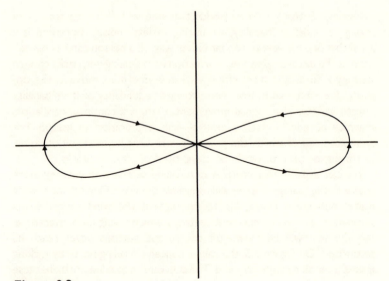

Figure 9.3
Movement of Meaning Search

tion to the familiar (banality)—seeking the new (good variety), and so on. Such a movement might look like a figure-eight lying on its side, as shown in Figure 9.3

However, as the metaphor of tacking implies, meaning-search is not mere random wandering, nor staggering from one extreme to another, but a skillful maneuvering and adaptive balancing between variety and redundancy (both needed)—ultimately a fine tuning.

This oscillatory view of meaning-search fits with Durkheim's view, already mentioned, that the anomic pursuit of novelties (variety) leads to boredom. It also fits with the finding of psychologists that moderate complexity is more interesting to people than is either extreme complexity or simplicity. The situation is suggested by an inverted U-curve, found by psychologists to apply to liking of complexity: there was most liking for moderate complexity, least for both high and low complexity (E. Walker, in Berlyne and Madsen [1973:68–69]). Turn such a curve right-side-up, and one has a picture of what I hypothesize is the situation with boredom: namely, that it is high at both ends of the continuum from monotony to variety, or from simplicity to complexity, while there

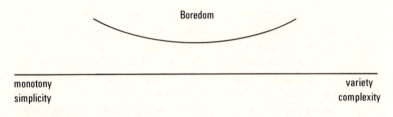

Figure 9.4
Bimodality of Boredom

is most interest and least boredom in the middle range, as suggested in Figure 9.4.

From this two-directional scheme, it follows that boredom doesn't all come from redundancy, as is often assumed, but also can come from variety. Nor do variety and excitement always relieve boredom. It depends on their significance to a receiver in the light of his needs and interests. Lack of significance is found at both extremes of experience labeled in our model as noise and banality. Boredom is bimodal.

A few examples from daily life can illustrate how variety and redundancy set bounds such as we have described for navigation in the sea of information. The limits of variety are less often seen than those of redundancy. Let us begin with some examples of how an overload of information can lose meaning and cause boredom. Everyone is familiar with the storyteller who cannot resist adding descriptive details that do not advance the story until he overwhelms his listeners with boredom from information—excessive variety. Said Voltaire, "The secret of being a bore is to tell everything."

A similar overload of variety happens in the experience known as museum fatigue. A person visits a museum with the best intentions of seeing it all with deep appreciation within an hour or so. But, to his surprise and embarrassment, for all his enthusiasm, his fatigue mounts, legs tire, and eyes glaze after seeing only a few halls full of treasures. There is no reason to doubt the sincerity of his interest. He suffers from an overload of information, a boredom resulting from the amount and variety, not the quality, of the information he tried to assimilate in a limited time. Of course, a hall full of identical exhibits would become boring for the opposite reason—not variety overload but monotony. The point is that degradation of meaning and boredom lie at both ends of the redundancy-variety (R-V) continuum.

A third example of the limit on variety comes from a game like tennis, whose (good) redundancy includes rules without which it could not be played. Players are restricted by the rules, but few would care to abolish them, for they make the game—its fun and meaning—possible. Play provides variety within these bounds. But suppose players wanting more variety were to relax the rules, allowing any number of players, allowing shots to land anywhere, removing the net, letting anyone serve whenever he pleases, varying the scoring method during a game—plainly it would turn into boring nonsense (bad variety) and the players would not keep it up long.

These examples show how variety, even of valuable information, can overwhelm interest and cause boredom when it goes too far and neglects the opposite direction of (good) redundancy.

Music well shows at both ends of the R-V continuum how loss of meaning can occur. As often noted, like a game, it has rules accepted by performers and listeners (scale, melody, harmony, rhythm, theme, score, composition, arrangement) which enable cooperation among performers and resonance with listeners to go on. Even forms of music that stress free improvisation—jazz, flamenco, rock, East Indian *ragas*—carry a load of redundancy that makes the genre recognizable and with whose familiarity the audience can resonate. Though improvisation aims at variety, it does so within this structure, expressed by the idea of improvisation upon a theme. Should it go too far beyond any recognizable theme, it risks becoming mere noise, to which the audience can attach no significance. But, on the other hand, the fading of popular songs and even hackneyed classics show how fast repetition (redundancy) can cause music to lose interest. At both ends of the R-V continuum meaning can be lost.

Let us now consider an example where redundancy is the main goal and not a bound one tries not to exceed. Traditional ceremonies repeat the meaning of the past; and, when this is important—for all their redundancy—they are not boring. Take, for example, a golden wedding anniversary. Its social function is to bring back warm memories and affirm bonds of kinship and friendship sustained over 50 years of married life. Strangers and novelty can make little contribution to such an event. Its purpose is good redundancy, to see the old familiar faces, and because of that function—despite lack of variety—it is interesting.

Another kind of social occasion may balance the high redundancy of an anniversary. A large cocktail party is a high-variety occasion, offering an adventure in meeting people. One "sails" into a crowd of strangers not so much to renew acquaintances as to find new opportunities for interaction. It would be somewhat of a letdown to meet only persons one knows well and sees every day. To be sure, even though variety is sought, there is possible boredom at that end too: in a motley crowd a high level of noise and irrelevance which one may endure without finding significant opportunities.

These two occasions succeed or fail for opposite reasons—the cocktail party aiming for production of variety that for a golden wedding anniversary would be noise—the golden wedding anniversary for redundancy that would be a bore at a cocktail party.

All of these examples—boring stories, museum fatigue, tennis, musical improvisation, a golden wedding anniversary, and a cocktail party— illustrate that redundancy and variety both function in every act of communication, but that at both ends of the R-V continuum there are bounds beyond which meaning is lost and redundancy and variety degrade into banality and noise, respectively—and boredom enters.

The meaningfulness of institutions, then, can be judged by how far in ensemble they balance good variety by good redundancy (and hold noise, banality, and boredom to a minimum). Here we get the connection that some institutions (in Chapter 10 called placebos) might compensate for low production of meaning by other institutions, by generating pseudo-redundancy (called by some sociologists pseudo-gemeinschaft) and pseudo-variety—pseudo-information (Chapter 7).

By the foregoing paradigm likening information search to the tacking of a ship against the wind of entropy, I have tried to express the main assumption of this book: that information can degrade under certain conditions.

Ordinarily people take for granted that knowledge is stable. But we know that on the physical side monuments erode, inks fade, books crumble, genes mutate (mostly nonadaptively). Need we suppose that entropy on the physical side is not paralleled by entropy on the symbolic? Let us make the opposite assumption that knowledge is unstable; that, like most things, it erodes and decays continually; that the tendency expressed in the second law of thermodynamics as dissipation of energy is also expressed as degradation of information. Structures of meaning, whatever and wherever they are, are subject to entropy no less than are physical structures.

Genetic information degrades relatively slowly, by mutation and cross-breeding. A few mutations are superior adaptations but most are useless and some are lethal (in the familiar case of fruit flies blind, wingless, sterile, and so on). Mutations and unselective cross-breeding are "noise" to the genotype or preferred breed.

Semantic information is that which is passed on by the meaning of symbols. Like culture, semantic information not only grows and changes but degrades much more rapidly than does genetic (Alfred Kroeber's point about the superorganic versus the organic). It is then a naive idea of progress that every accumulation of information is a step forward. Not only does knowledge have destructive applications, but it itself degrades naturally and continually. The size of the heap of information is no guarantee against this. T.S. Eliot's famous plaint about wisdom lost in knowledge and knowledge lost in information is one expression of this. The fact seems to be that the mind (therefore culture) is a leaky bucket. Psychologists' curves of memory show rapid early forgetting. Ideas degenerate into clichés, and stereotypes (Ortega y Gasset, 1932; Lippman, 1922; Zijderveld, 1979). News reporting is selective and slanted. Rumors undergo leveling and other distortions (Allport and Postman, 1947). Ritual becomes formalism (Cooley, 1927), and faith hardens into dogma. Fashions lose significance and fade (Chapter 5). On a larger scale, the decline of art styles, religions, and even whole civilizations has been portrayed by thinkers such as Toynbee (1947) and Sorokin (1941). From such considerations, to assume that information degrades, culturally and individually, is not unrealistic.

Nor—if degradation is a natural tendency of information—is it unreasonable to suppose that more processing does not necessarily improve information. On the contrary, the more information is repeated and duplicated, the larger the scale of diffusion, the greater the speed of processing, the more opinion leaders and gatekeepers and networks, the more filtering of messages, the more kinds of media through which information is passed, the more decoding and encoding, and so on—the more degraded information might be. As with energy transformation, greater throughput of information may merely increase its entropy—an idea admirably expressed by Kohr (1977) as diseconomy of scale, and specifically in terms of entropy of energy by Georgescu-Roegen (1971), Henderson (1978), and Rifkin (1980). Because of such degradation, I hypothesize that although the amount of information in modern culture has increased vastly, the meaning of that information has not—indeed, modern society is suffering what is acknowledged to be a meaning crisis.

Having stated the idea of degradation of information in terms of a metaphor of a ship tacking but drifting into "losing" areas called noise and banality, let me now try to put it into more literal terms of communication. In terms of communication, the navigator on the sea of information in the metaphor is now a receiver coping with an environment in which information coming to him is more or less degraded. If information is defined as reduction of a receiver's uncertainty about any state of affairs (such as a signal, message, or source of information), then degradation of information is any way in which signals tell less to reduce receiver's uncertainty about such affairs.

As implied by the ship metaphor, information degrades in two main ways. One is by acting like noise. We define noise as any signal or stimulus that increases the receiver's uncertainty about a state of affairs because it interferes with (competes with, distracts from, blurs or confuses)—hence precludes—better information from the same channel. So equivocation, to the extent that it creates uncertainty about a message, is noiselike. Because it is an expression of entropy, noise continually encroaches all channels. It may consist of nonsense (random variety) or signals that carry some other information than receiver wants, that is, information in one context is perfectly capable of acting as noise in another.

So, in an information-flooded society such as ours, we view the receiver as continually decoding information from a rather adverse environment. Much is garbled. Much is buried in codes he cannot read. Much is manipulated to distort his interpretation. It is a world where chaotic events continually defy orderly interpretation. (Any day's news should suffice to illustrate such a point.) Among the costs of high social noise are difficulty in attaining resonance, finding meaning, and clearly defining style and identity. "High noise" level, then, describes a situation which, however fact-filled, is not functioning to guide people to destinations but presenting obstacles to their courses.

Let us briefly list some ways in which information in our media system degrades by becoming more noiselike and increasing the noise/signal ratio: (1) degradation from psychological sources (forgetting of message, code or signal; distortion from mind of decoder, encoder or transmitter [imagination, fantasy, hallucination, bias] error of encoding or decoding); (2) amplification becomes noise when volume of one signal increases at cost of other equally valuable or interesting signals; (3) difficulty of decoding makes it harder to get meaning from, especially exogenous, signals; (4) irrelevance: information is so disconnected and diverse that receiver has difficulty finding a significant pattern or code by which to decipher; (5) equivocation and ambiguity increase receiver's uncertainty about messages; (6) rather than reducing receiver's uncertainty, communication reflects the complicatedness and confusion ("bad" complexity) of society; (7) channel clutter: too many messages in crowded channels act like noise; (8) dearth of feedback is a deprivation in seeming abundance of information; (9) stylistic noise makes it harder to find and support identity (by good redundancy); (10) signals purport to carry information but in fact do not (pseudo-information); (11) manipulation of information (hype) decreases receiver's certainty about, and control over, the actual state of affairs; and (12) sheer overload: the larger the volume of communication, or faster the input of information, the greater is the likelihood that it will act as noise to any signal.

The other main way that information degrades in modern society was described as banalization, an overload of sameness, in other words, loss of information from repetition past the point of functional redundancy. Like noise, banality not only has little to say but gets in the way of more significant messages. It can be trivial or sententious. Because it lacks functional redundancy, it interferes with social resonance. Because it cuts off information, it gives people a sense of being insulated, cocooned, sealed, trapped.

Some common ways in which information degrades into banality may be listed: (1) psychological sources: forgetting, habituation; (2) leveling: loss of detail in repeating or copying information: rumors, cheap duplication (kitsch); (3) mechanical, monotonous repetition, as in mass production of goods; (4) uniform diffusion by media of popular culture; (5) fashion imitation (loss of information proved by rapid fading); (6) gatekeepers restricting information available to closed group or network; (7) cultural over-filtering, which gives a sense of being cut off from nature, reality, or authenticity; and (8) institutions (social placebos) that offer consolation as compensation for boredom or lack of meaning.

Why do so much noise and banality grow up in modern society? An obvious reason seems to be that they are easier to make than meaningful signals. Rapid change favors noise. In the case of banality, it is economical—one might say lazier—to repeat and imitate than to make something. But beneath that is the fundamental point, I think, that entropy—of which noise and banality are expressions—has a natural tendency to increase. Like rust, it takes no effort; and one must guard against it all the time. If, as Wiener put it, we are in a Niagara of entropy, then failing to pull at the oars is sufficient to explain drifting downstream. Noise expresses variety flooding to the point of disorder; banality shows uniformatization, leveling, stagnation, creeping to the point of loss of potential for growth and discovery. Because of these opposed and variable tendencies, society does not hold a steady course within the functional range of variety and redundancy but drifts (wanders, staggers, oscillates) between overloads of noise and banality.

But there is another element in the picture, which acts to damp such veerings and stabilize the social system by assuaging and reducing awareness of tensions such as boredom. Let us consider the hypothesis that certain institutions can act as antidotes for boredom and discontent, by giving meaning to compensate for boredom; and, doing so, mask the actual amount of meaninglessness in our information society.

10

SOCIAL PLACEBOS

Civilization carries its pain but also its Novocain. In this chapter we look at activities that give meaning to compensate for the meaning missing in institutions. So they relieve tensions such as boredom and frustration, which otherwise might threaten the stability of the social system. However, they do not remedy sources of tension but merely make people feel better about an unsatisfactory state of affairs. For this reason they might be called social placebos. They keep people off the streets; they keep them watching television and lotteries; they inflate dreams. So consoling and diverting us, social placebos foster false consciousness such as ideology. It is possible that some institutions work like stage props, helping the show to go on even when it is on the verge of a failure of confidence.

Where does such an idea come from? The origin of placebos may go as far back as that of magic; but the first deliberate large-scale use of entertainment as a placebo seems to have originated with the ancient Romans during the age of Augustus. Their gladiatorial games gave idle soldiers work and kept the populace so preoccupied with sensational spectacles and so pleased with the generosity of their rulers that they did not realize how badly they were governed. It was perhaps the first time that an entertainment institution had been deliberately used as a sort of sop to placate people and keep them in a state of contented deception.

It does not take much imagination to find parallels between the Roman games and modern media and sport spectacles. The movie "Roller Ball" (1977) portrayed a multinational corporation ruling the world, using bloody roller derbies to entertain and catharsize the tensions of subject populations in Japan, America, and elsewhere. Long before that, Aldous Huxley (1932) and George Orwell (1949) had envisaged totalitarian societies using sophisticated placebos for control: in the former drugs and orgiastic ritual, and in the latter even televised fake wars to build morale.

But there is no reason to suppose that placebo institutions are confined to totalitarian regimes. Democracies have use for them, too. Take television give-away game shows. A critic (Meyer, 1978) says, "Participants gurgle and squeal with almost orgasmic ecstasy as goodies are flashed before them, and the winners gape like zombies at the loot they have acquired. Around 40 million Americans regularly watch these shows and salivate." Is it not plausible to suppose that such give-aways could be consoling people for something they are not getting in real, daily life?

The general idea is not of a device imposed on people but of an institution that may have grown up naturally, which works in one way or another to ease tensions without remedying and sometimes by hiding them. Well-meaning people may devise placebos, and a majority choose them. Nevertheless, all placebos do serve stability, and that could be to the benefit of some special group.

The systemic view calls attention to the connections among things. Thinking of society as a system, the function of a placebo might be likened to that of a pump on a leaky ship, while water in the hold represents the level of social tensions. The rate of pumping offsets the rise of water in the hold; the more the ship leaks, the faster the pump works. Were it not for the pump, the ship would soon go down. But the pump slows down as the level of water falls, so the ship never gets rid of the water in the hold. If I might add one more detail to the metaphor, the sound of the pump sometimes lulls the passengers into a sense of false prosperity, that all is well, or that they are going somewhere when in fact the motor is stalled and the ship is drifting. Applying this to society, one might say that social problems and poorly working institutions contribute to the level of tension. But other institutions help relieve tensions they are not really remedying. I call the latter placebos. Recognizing that a placebo does not eliminate tension any more than a pump does the leak in the hold, does not necessarily argue that it is false and should be gotten rid of. Don't knock placebo if that is all one has.

Perhaps the oldest explicit formulation of the idea of the social placebo was Plato's, of myths used by an elite to keep the rest of the people content. It was all for the good of everybody, of course. Catharsis, an important component of placebo institutions, was recognized by Aristotle, who analyzed how poetry and drama purge emotions.

Machiavelli gave the idea of placebo a more cynical twist: To keep people's minds off disturbing topics, the ruler should give honors and art prizes, and divert the populace with festivals and shows. It is easy to win popular favor by such hype, as we would now call it, for "the vulgar is always taken by appearances." (*The Prince*, XVIII, XXI).

Another twist to the placebo idea came from two nineteenth-century thinkers who attacked religion on grounds that it was acting on people like a drug. Nietzsche said Christianity was a servile doctrine by which the weak and lowly overcame a superior class by inducing the latter to give up their natural strength for virtues such as humility, love, and equality. Marx charged the ruling class with imposing ideology through institutions such as education, the press, the courts—and especially religion, the "opium of the people." Contemporary Marxists now often apply the "opium of the people" idea to mass media, consumers' goods, and popular culture, their reason being, as one would expect, that capitalistic domination is the reason for it (Real, 1977:25; Gorz, 1967:94; Marcuse, 1964:79, 84).

Freud went further with the idea that certain elements of mental and social life disguise realities and make people more comfortable. He showed how goals are substituted and disguised; mental processes such as rationalization, sublimation, and projection allow acceptable release of suppressed impulses; and some institutions—art, religion, courts, education, psychotherapy—are especially concerned with easing tensions such as guilt and anxiety.

William James's (1911) idea of a "moral equivalent of war" (earlier used by Gandhi in 1906 to describe *Satygraha* [Easwaran, 1978:161]) was a more pointed statement of how institutions might substitute for war by providing outlets for more acceptable forms of aggression, such as sport or struggle for reform. James argued that it was a waste of time to seek universal peace and disarmament because "the plain truth" was that aggressiveness is unavoidable and "people want war," but it would be possible to "invent new outlets for heroic energy" that would be more useful, such as conscripting an army to fight poverty (an idea finally launched by Franklin D. Roosevelt in 1933 as the Civilian Conservation Corps).

Safety-valve institutions became the term preferred by sociologists and anthropologists for an institution like a carnival, which seems especially designed to release tensions—allow people to escape from ordinary restrictions, let go, and enjoy in a sublimated form behavior that otherwise might be condemned—all of which was a compensation for restrictions or deprivations the rest of the time. Talcott Parsons (1951:304–308) described a safety-valve institution as part of a social system. Sociologist Coser (1956:151–156) analyzed how various sorts of conflict could displace hostility and so benefit cohesion by drawing off hostilities that otherwise might be directed within the group. So could ritual rebellion, as in clowning, mummery, burlesque, Halloween mischief, and status reversal, be seen as catharsis for tension generated by social structure: while such "rites of reversal obviously include a protest against the established order . . . they are intended to preserve and strengthen the established order" (Gluckman, 1965:109). Likewise, emotional compensations have been found in gambling (Tec, 1964), or in religious revivalism among the poor (Pope, 1942) for a lack of economic and social status rewards. However, such functions are not manifest, as sociologists understand these terms (Merton, 1968), but latent. Therefore, they are not directly observed but require sophisticated inference—and, as might be expected, considerable dispute about just what is happening (Babcock, ed., 1978:22–25, 206–207).

Rather than use these ideas—safety valve and opium—so troubled by controversy, I prefer the term social placebo, because it covers a broader spectrum of consolations for institutions that do not work well and because it opens a new dimension of the safety-valve idea: the power of suggestion to supply almost anything that is imagined.

What is a social placebo? It is an institution, practice, or product that consoles us for something wrong or lacking, in ways similar to that of a medical placebo. Let us, then, look first at a medical placebo. Better known as a pink pill, a placebo is a substance or procedure used with a patient as part of treatment that works by hope and suggestion rather than real medicinal effects—"Anything lacking intrinsic remedial value, done or given to humor another" (*American Heritage Dictionary*, Houghton Mifflin). Most doctors readily admit using placebos, if more effective treatment is lacking, and because they really work. Many experimental studies show large placebo effects on such conditions as anxiety, pain, pulse rate, gastric acid levels, bleeding ulcers, arthritis, and Parkinson's disease (Cousins, 1977). About 30 percent of the healing of proven drugs comes from placebo effect. Even better results—36 percent—come from placebos used to relieve pain (Goodwin, 1979). Hypnosis, widely used in therapy (Kroger, 1963), shows the power of a suggested image to erase pain of a real injury, even make one see something that is not there.

A perfectly designed medical placebo would have a full spectrum of suggestive effects, such as (1) assurances of a physician in whom the patient has confidence; (2) testimonials of people who have benefited from it; (3) impressive design, package, color (British researchers found red more effective than blue, green, or yellow as a color for pills [Bishop, 1977]), and so on; (4) palliative effects (pain-killing, sedating, tension-reducing, tranquilizing, anti-depressant, or whatever); (5) give a reward (sugary syrup, alcohol)—even a high, euphoria—as a bonus; (6) divert the patient from unhappiness and despair, give him something to do (regimen, exercise, craft) that sustains hope; and (7) real healing through the power of suggestion.

To be sure, a placebo works fully only if the patient is deceived, benignly of course. It is given by someone who knows about it to someone who doesn't know and isn't told. By such ignorance and suggestion of something that isn't so at the time, the patient enjoys a happier state of mind than he would otherwise.

Much of this, I say, can be transferred to institutions. Perhaps the most important point is that an institution can compensate—make up—for something else that is lacking, just as a medical placebo can take the place of more effective treatment. Compensation finds something else (Y) to take the place of X that is lacking, though normally available or originally preferable.

In particular, four features of medical placebos can, I suggest, be transferred to social institutions and policies. (1) The placebo serves in lieu of a better remedy for something that is wrong or lacking in institutions. (2) The placebo consoles or relieves a receiver in some way, such as by catharsis (such as an ombudsman helps people to "sound off," apart from whatever practical good he achieves). (3) The placebo produces real results merely by faith or suggestion. (4) The placebo works by or contributes to false consciousness of the beneficiary, such as diverting attention from something that is wrong. (If a receiver recognizes a political placebo, he may call it tokenism.) It is less often a matter of finding a pure social placebo than of how far valid institutions, that may have proved themselves by years of service, take on such functions.

Magic approaches the requirements of a perfect social placebo, because it uses ritual (in place of effective means) to console the practitioner and also produce real results by the autosuggestive power of a vivid image and faith that it will work. Well-known anthropological studies show how sorcery works for people who really believe in it (Fortune, 1932; Warner, 1937; Evans-Pritchard, 1937). Who can doubt that magic functions in our own society, too, where it is a big business of millions of dollars in charms, love potions, horoscopes, fortune telling, prophecies, seances, and so on. Witchcraft has thousands of followers in England and North America, performing rituals for worldly success. The health field is also pervaded by magic: regimens of diet, exercise, exercise gadgets, wonder foods, miracle drugs; health food stores with racks of books making startling claims; psychological gadgets sold by mail; faith-healing methods, many of which are frankly hypnotic; and health spas giving rosy pictures of renovation by exercises, cosmetics, diets, waters, spartan discipline, and treatments such as a "holy Ganges ritual." Practical success and prosperity-training seminars also use the magic of suggestion, teaching students to think positively (because "ideas become true") and repeat formulas like, "I am a rich and wondrous being" (one asks students to face the class and jump up and down, shouting "Whooo-eee! I see abundance everywhere!"). Some, indeed, do make money, helped by autosuggestion; and those who do not make money keep themselves pleasantly occupied by dreams of it.

Religion also may fall under suspicion of being a placebo when it is used to justify an earthly institution, for there are no God-ordained armies, courts, banks, bureaucracies—they are all made by people. Religion may be suspected of acting as a placebo also when it stresses magical prayer for success, healing, and miracles; emotional catharsis (revivalism, speaking in tongues, group confession, and the like); resignation toward troubles; ritual in place of practical action; salvation in place of success; retreat into monasteries; focus on another world to come. Well-known studies of sects and cults (Pope, 1942; Wilson, 1961; Lanternari, 1963; Lewis, 1971; Sargent, 1973) show that they do indeed offer such consolations to people who are not well off otherwise. The boom of cults today may indicate a turning of more people to placebos.

However, a doctrinaire indictment of religion as a placebo is not justified. First, there is no necessity to admit that placebos are categorically bad. Second, it is a question of to what extent functions of placebo actually are taking the place of genuine services. These are *options*, not necessities. It cannot be denied that some churches have become entrenched in power structures, opposed to reform, even active partners in domination. On the other hand, many religions have been agents of change—a Father Berrigan, Pastor Niemoller, John Woolman, or Mahatma Gandhi can hardly be convicted of consoling people with illusion, making them passive, and diverting criticism from social structure and action from this world. Sects such as Jehovah's Witnesses and Quakers have given deep challenge to military conscription and loyalty to the state. Where, then, are the placebos? I think one will find more of them in those bland popular religions that give no challenge to the political-economic structure, encourage moneymaking and worldly success, and compete with entertainment industries like Disney for audiences and box office and media ratings.

Let us look at some more contemporary institutions whose functions seem in one way or another to fit the picture of a social placebo. I see four categories: (1) institutions that offer or deliver toys, baubles, prizes, tokens, or fetishes that could be called material consolations; (2) drugs or foods that console by bio-chemical action; (3) activity outlets; and (4) vicarious consolations.

MATERIAL CONSOLATIONS

One sort of institution that deserves to be suspected of being a placebo is that which delivers—or dangles a promise of—payoffs that are like prizes one wins at a carnival: toys, baubles, gaudy trinkets. Giveaway games on television fit such a description. So also does advertising, with its bountiful promise of consumer goods. It is not hard to see the endless succession of fads and novelties spun out by the merchandising system as rather like prizes from a carnival wheel, consoling us with baubles for other things we may not be getting, though a psychological reckoning is difficult. Social critic Melvin Maddocks (1978) asks whether we have:

turned into a nation of intellectual disco-dancers, waiting for the next flash of strobe-light, the next heavy beat—choosing to be informed only about a world made up of Jackie O., astrology charts, and the latest fashionable drug. . . . Maybe as our history grows more serious we are . . . growing more trivial, retreating into a funhouse of toys and games. . . .

Even more bountiful in promises is gambling, which can hardly fail to come to mind as a practice that, like magic, offers rewards for nothing, dreams of easy wealth that can console those who otherwise have failed, and seems ideally suited to be a social placebo. It is deeply institutionalized in modern life, a growing pastime, approved and indulged in by well over half the American people, of whom some 15 million are illegal and 4 million addicted (compulsive) gamblers. It thrives in state-run lotteries, casinos (California, Las Vegas, Reno, Atlantic City), race tracks, legal offtrack betting facilities, illegal handbooks, cardrooms, arcades, taverns, bingo parlors, and churches. Establishment in such institutions would make it extremely hard to get rid of gambling—if many wanted to (less than one-fifth of Americans do).

Kaplan (1979) claims that sports provide the major vehicle for gambling to escape the tedium of modern jobs and that proliferation of legalized gambling as a consequence of boredom in the world of work diverts public attention from critical social issues and methods for handling them. Gambling is effective in combatting boredom because it can dramatize the trivial—make an issue and create consequences in events that have none inherently.

Beyond relief from boredom and dreams of easy wealth, gambling gives other consolations such as Felicia Campbell (1976) found among slot-machine players at Las Vegas: thrilling "involvement," release from tension, and a sense of equality to many (such as the aged) who would otherwise be defeated by modern life. Slot-machine play can also compensate for loneliness, according to one old lady who said that the blinking lights and ringing bells on the payoffs seem to say, "I like you." Campbell argues that, because of such consolations, such gambling is beneficial, even therapeutic, and should be retained as a humanizing institution. Nechama Tec (1964) found similar functions for Swedes from soccer pools, especially for people of the upper part of the lower class, who aspired to something better yet were restricted by a status gap between manual work and white-collar or commercial success. For people so blocked, "wagering keeps alive dreams."

The hopes provided by gambling, although almost never realized, tend to make a deprivational situation less acute and less urgent. . . . Instead of turning against the original source of their deprivations and unfulfilled aspirations, bettors are relieved through gambling of some of the frustrations and, hence, are less likely to attack the existing class structure (Tec, 1964:108, 113–114).

Gambling runs and thrives on false consciousness. Magical elements help it to function and make it more fun: belief in hunches; prophecies of touts and prognosticators; betting systems; betting on lucky colors, numbers, machines, "hot" jockeys, or players with "runs" of good luck; especially vain dreams (one state-run lottery advertises in television and newspapers, "someone will win a million dollars at the end of your rainbow"; in New York a newspaper advertisement shows a king, with the caption "a chance to live like me"); and a belief of each in his own luck though the aggregate lose (in the Atlantic City casino a "take" of $600,000 per day, with losses of $18 per hour per player during the summer of 1978). One can see that gambling, giveaway contests, and get-rich sales pitches foster an ideology of something for nothing, in which easy money replaces hard work and a dream of riches consoles for inflation and rising taxes. So gambling approaches a perfect placebo with many compensations such as diverting activity; excitement, relief from boredom, catharsis of the occasional win or hit, dream of wealth, and other rewards (such as status of a "high roller" or "hustler"); and serving false consciousness by keeping vain hope alive and fostering magical faith. Not only that, but when gambling is deliberately used as a way of collecting easy tax dollars and gaining popularity with voters (for not taxing in other ways), it is hard not to see the resemblance to the Roman games.

CHEMICAL PLACEBOS

A dock worker in Lima, Peru, chews coca leaves while carrying 200-pound bales on his back because it makes life as well as his work easier for him; he is less aware of his hard lot. I call substances that when ingested work bio-chemically to dull pain, relieve tension, or give pleasurable kicks, chemical placebos when they are used as consolation or escape.

Huge industries, legal and illegal, are busy supplying chemical placebos, of which alcohol is most popular. In the United States there are an estimated 9 to 10 million alcoholics and alcohol abusers. Other countries such as Scandinavia and Iceland use even more; the Soviet Union estimates that it loses 10 percent of production per year because of alcoholism (Willis, 1978). France leads the world in alcohol consumption—each year the equivalent of 25 gallons of wine, 10 gallons of beer, and 2.5 gallons of hard liquor and brandy per person (Dowell, 1980). Australians spend one dollar on drink for every three dollars they spend on food, almost half the men and 58 percent of the women admitting a "dangerous level" of drinking, especially among women the drinking is attributed to boredom (Deeley, 1978).

Aside from alcohol, tranquilizers are the most heavily used legal drugs in America. Five *billion* are prescribed annually in the U.S., according to the Food and Drug Adminstration (FDA) (1980). Valium (known as the "happiness pill") is taken by an estimated 25 million persons (U.S. National Institute of Drug Abuse, 1975), spending over a half billion dollars per year. Doctors in the United States in 1971 wrote enough prescriptions for mood-altering drugs, says psychiatrist Mitchell S. Rosenthal, "to keep every man, woman and child...either 'up,' 'down' or 'out of it' for a solid month."

Pot (marijuana) heads the list of illegal tranquilizers used by younger persons; one in eleven high school seniors smoke the latter *daily* (Jones, 1978); a sociological study of working-class youth (Schwartz et al., 1973) reported pot widely used, on or off the job, to escape from boredom; "not having at least half a 'joint' in the morning casts gloom over the day." In the military, also, drugs are widely used. According to a report of a congressional subcommittee, following interviews with about 1,000 enlisted men and officers, drug use is a way of life for men in uniform. On bases the ideal for many is to stay "stoned," a military policeman claiming to have achieved that feat for three months.

Vigorous campaigns against drug abuse, military and civilian, do little to reduce alcohol advertising and the large part that chemical placebos play in modern life.

ACTIVE OUTLETS

The Greeks of the town of Patras are good-spirited and well mannered, but once a year a strange madness breaks out among them. During the weekend before Lent, as part of a carnival with merrymaking, colorful costumes, parades, music in the streets, and throwing confetti, a sort of playful warfare breaks out. Everyone, young and old, arms himself with a plastic hammer or bat and bops anyone within reach; no one can avoid being bopped on the head. Saturday evening, after the children are put to bed, the fighting grows fiercer; gangs emerge; some of the more aggressive boppers put on helmets; even restaurants are not safe as customers and waiters throw confetti, burst balloons on heads, and wield bats and hammers. Monday all the silliness stops, the decorations are taken down; "purged of aggressions, everyone packs up his weapons and drives home" (Prasinos, 1978).

It should be possible for anyone to agree, without elaborate theorizing, that there is an aggressive outlet in such activity that has nothing specifically to do with the particular person being bopped—though that does not rule out occasionally settling a score. On the whole, the carnival is plainly fun, and one can easily imagine that were the rest of one's life rather dull and restrained, that carnival would be a high point of self-expression and play consoling oneself for dullness the rest of the time. Much more could be debated about the meaning of the bopping and of the carnival, but at least it illustrates what I would call an active outlet, a letting go of energy and tension in ways beyond what the rules usually allow.

It is easy to think of other institutions in the same category, such as the revelry, mummery, masquerading, dancing, and clowning of the carnival of Rio de Janeiro or the Mardi Gras of New Orleans. Bopping also has some resemblance to Halloween mischief, and it is not far away from the pranks of April Fool's Day, explosives of the Fourth of July, and the noise and drinking binges of New Year's Eve. Fiestas in Mexico and Latin America are sometimes highly expressive, exploding firecrackers as on our Fourth of July. Bopping is also similar to comedy that allows one to insult somebody by pranks and degradations of the sort suffered by Falstaff or a circus clown falling into a trough of wet plaster; or an amusement park concession allowing one for a dollar to throw baseballs at a clown sitting on a collapsible seat that dumps him into the water when a ball strikes a lever.

All such arrangements give license to behavior not ordinarily allowed, for people under the guise of fun to let go energetically and physically—to get something off their chests or out of their systems. Indeed, the success of festivals such as the Fourth of July, New Year's Eve, Halloween, and All Fool's Day is judged by how enthusiastically people let off steam. I call such institutions that seem to aim at physical catharsis active outlets.

However, it is not the sheer amount of exercise or energy expended that makes an activity cathartic. For example, football is not necessarily more cathartic than a less exhausting sport. Rather, it is *spending tension that comes from somewhere else.* Nor is it that an institution permits certain behavior not allowed somewhere else (such as tackling people only on a football field), since most institutions have such limitations. Rather, it is the amount of spontaneous emotional letting go (some games unexpectedly turn out to be highly cathartic, while others of the same sport do not).

The conception of catharsis used here is the ordinary one of emotional purging or letting go that brings satisfaction or relief. Catharsis can be active, as in carnivals; or vicarious—a sort of emotional hitchhiking on the affairs of others. This definition is, therefore, broader than, and inclusive of, Scheff's (1980:67) definition of catharsis as properly distanced discharge of distresses of grief, fear, anger, and embarrassment.

Primitive forms of religion stressing rhythm, trance, exhaustion, even orgy, are good examples of catharsis. They aim at ecstasy, not exercise. Voodoo dancing, for example, creates a hypnotic trance with an abreactive catharsis (Sargent, 1973). Or take the active outlet described in this scene from an early Kentucky camp meeting:

At one time, at least 500 were swept down, overcome by religious frenzy, the "slain of the Lord" taken with the "falling exercise," some lying unconscious, others shouting and screaming; others rolled and tumbled in the mud clutching their knees, others were stricken by the "jerks," in which caps and bonnets would fly off and the loose hair of women "would crack almost as loud as a wagoner's whip"; others were afflicted by the "holy laugh," or would run on all fours and bark (R. Wallace, 1955:71).

Clowning often functions to vent community blame and judgment, perhaps saved up from many events. For example, Hopi Indian clowns, called mudheads, come forth during Kachina festivals to make fun of members with whom the community finds fault. Some sort of mockery, if only joking, is found in all societies, to ease tensions and make everyone, except the victim, feel better. In Eskimo drum duels, men who have quarreled taunt each other and air grievances in song for the amusement of the assembled community. Likewise, in the ancient Athenian comedy, leaders such as Pericles and Socrates were lampooned. Nor is this very different from the annual gridiron banquets in Washington, D.C., in which newsmen burlesque the President and other invited officials who must endure it all with good humor. From such examples, we see that the jester is not a mere prankster but a sort of group spokesperson whose jibes give comic catharsis to grievance, blame, and criticism.

Another thing that cathartic outlets do is help people bear authority. For example, in Japan at year's end, saki parties are often held in which male employees sit on equal terms with the boss. After prolonged conversation and imbibement, supposedly under the influence of alcohol, etiquette relaxes and the employees begin to speak their minds in criticisms and complaints that they would never think of voicing under normal circumstances. The boss accepts these remarks without loss of face and is supposed not to hold a grudge. Such catharsis for underdogs presumably contributes to the paternalism and corporate warmth so notable in Japanese industrial life. A fascinating variant of underdog catharsis is found among the Ndembu of Zambia, who mock their new chief *before* he is installed, presumably in anticipation of what they will have to put up with from him after he becomes chief, to have their last fling and chasten his pride in authority. He is ceremonially humiliated, sitting with bowed head, "the pattern of all patience" (V. Turner, 1969:100–102).

It is not necessary to prove that the tension level of society is actually reduced by cathartic outlets. It is plain they do give relief, however temporary; and in that way, if no other, help compensate people for what they must put up with. In some cases one can see the grievance or deprivation that is the source of tension; in others one can only conjecture what accounts of tension are being drawn upon. Psychologists agree that feelings can be displaced from forgotten causes. So it is reasonable to suppose that a carnival provides legitimate outlets for outbursts that might otherwise take less desirable forms, such as riots, vandalism, graffiti because such substitution (sublimation) reduces challenge to the existing order. The main point is that cathartic outlets compensate people for something that might otherwise be lacking or wrong in the rest of life. The higher the tension level, the more need there is, presumably, for such outlets.

For such reasons, one may expect them to be deliberately used as political safety valves. In this light one may look at the huge sports programs of East Germany and other Soviet bloc countries, so heavily subsidized in the midst of lack of consumer goods.

A line of dance crazes from Discomania to the Charleston and Black Bottom comes quickly to mind as energetic outlets that could well be compensating for something else lacking from people's lives. The International Discotheque Association estimated that the 10,000 American discos took in an average $7,000 per week with customers spending an average of five to ten dollars a night; the annual national investment being of the order of $5 billion. One discotheque manager said, "They go to discos not just to forget money problems, but to forget all problems." Escape to a different identity seems to be a compensatory function of disco-dancing, reminiscent of carnival masquerade, as explained by Rachel Zylberberg, founder of the discotheque movement in Paris:

When people come to my club, they want to take on another identity, to think they're somebody else. It's very important to give them the feeling of being somebody different. Everybody wants to be a somebody—especially the nobodys (Nevin, 1979).

Pinball arcades and pool halls substitute for sports programs and employment. They are supposed by some merchants to hold vandalism down, by others to increase it. Managers of pinball arcades characterize their clientele as bored juveniles (aged 12 to 22). Players say the arcades give an opportunity to meet friends and provide "fun when there is nothing else to do."

The fad of coin-operated electronic video games (Pac Man, Space Invaders, Demon Video, and the like) which erupted among Americans in 1981–82, seems to have a placebo function of relieving boredom by substitute activity. Arcades, doughnut shops, malls, and the like became centers crowded with avid teenagers working video games. *Time* magazine estimated that Americans dropped 20 to 28 billion quarters into video games in 1981—an amount surpassing all the money grossed by films, records, and sports—a total of 75,000 person-years playing, not including play on home video sets (Norton, 1982). Groups such as the Parent Teacher Association (PTA), concerned about moral effects of such "addiction," tried by ordinances to regulate, even prohibit, video-game playing by teenagers—apparently ignoring the real questions of what it was about institutions such as school that induced boredom and whether there were not worse alternatives if video games were not available.

Another example of activity outlet is "playing war," a regular event in San Diego County, in which about 20 teenagers fight with bamboo staffs, in military uniforms or camouflage fatigues, under conditions simulating real war. A participant described the cathartic experience as follows: "When we're out here, you're mind is off everything . . . all your problems. Your mind is on (playing) war. It's hard to describe why we like it. . . . You are out here with friends and you're laughing, you're singing" (Pund, 1985).

Market activity can be cathartic when it takes the form of splurges and binges in which one lets go from normal restraint. Buying binges are an important ritual of consumer society: mountains of goods, credit cards, and expense accounts invite splurging in wining and dining, vacations, buying cars, and so on. Such excitement in some measure consoles people for humdrum living the rest of the time.

VICARIOUS CATHARSIS

Catharsis need not be active. Merely watching people do things can be cathartic, too; indeed, there is striking economy in the fact that 100,000 people in a stadium can get a thrill out of one man's motion. Vicarious catharsis is emotional fulfillment from the role of somebody else—not a service he delivers but satisfaction of fantasy from putting oneself imaginatively into his shoes, to share his triumphs and fate, which social psychologists often call role-taking, identification, or vicarious experience.

A popular fantasy figure, whether living, historical, fictional, or legendary, enacts a fantasy of how people like to think of themselves, lifting them from a reality that may be humdrum or sordid. This public role corresponds only weakly to reality (whatever that is). For some its function is to provide a hero model to strive to be like; but for more it merely compensates for what they do not or cannot do—adding a fantasy dimension of meaning to life.

With such a function in mind, a movie actress, Raquel Welch—a fantasy figure herself—comments on the public roles of the president and first lady:

King Reagan and Queen Nancy, they're just a couple of TV stars.... American politics is all like Disneyland and if things get dull you can always call in the Marines.... The Reagans are just fantasy figures. Well, I'm one of those myself. ... I've been inside make-believe all my life and I know the Americans are being sold fantasy. Our politics really are a TV soap, like the Olympic Games (Mortimer, 1984:10).

One way or another, most of us add meaning to our lives by vicarious participation. This is a prime function of fiction and theater. Sports spectacles, such as Rose Bowl and Super Bowl games and the World Series are important to millions today. Eugene Ionesco (1980) said: "In France, everyone, rich and poor alike, is completely absorbed for a month each year by the *Tour Cycliste*, and the rest of the time, on Sundays anyway, by French soccer and rugby matches." A Japanese football fan says, "Watching and playing football offers a chance to be spontaneous—to let our emotions loose—which is often lacking in Japan's conformist society. It gives us a chance to yell and fight."

However, when sports enjoyment turns into extreme emotion—as in contests in which people gnash their teeth and scream, "Kill the umpire!" "Murder the bums!" (as might be seen in violent sports like professional wrestling and roller derbies), it is plainly letting go tensions that have been accumulated somewhere else in life and could not possibly be justified by the trivial issue of whether A or B displays more athletic skill. Such displacement compensates people for frustrations received elsewhere.

Or take the case of a film that not only gives enjoyment but acts as an emotional sop. Such was the "Sound of Music," an all-time hit, which from its first showing produced a "fantastic cult," seen by over 35,000,000 people in the first two years, some seeing it dozens of times, a hundred times, and one lady 810 times (Shearer, 1966). What it seems to have given people was not only musical enjoyment but consolation by feelings warmer than their own real life: emotional compensation.

Another example of vicarious placebo is paperback books supplying romantic escape to women. Harlequin romances, for example, having 14 percent of the American and 28 percent of the Canadian market, sell $100 million worth of love stories per year, of which the average reader buys six of the twelve new titles a month. They take women to a faraway place for a love affair, in which "violent, passionate kisses always end up just this side of the bedroom door" (Levine, 1977). So vicarious catharsis can console people for what is lacking in ordinary life, such as frustrations and humdrum living.

Three institutions of modern life especially deserve scrutiny as veritable Christmas trees loaded with vicarious placebos: entertainment media, the pantheon of celebrities, and the fantasy world of Disney. Entertainment media are loaded with placebos because they are cybernetically organized, through the market and box office and audience ratings, to supply whatever pleases most people. One can imagine what would happen if a hospital laid out medicines in a sort of cafeteria. Those most attractively colored, best tasting, giving the best "high," quickly relieving symptoms, and with fewest unpleasant side-effects, would soon become the standard pharmaceutical bill-of-fare. Because they manufacture dreams to fit popular wishes (Powdermaker, 1951), mass media have long been recognized by communication experts as "social narcotics" (Schramm, 1973:238–239). Of all placebos, television may prove the greatest, the main entertainment for adults (who keep it on over seven hours per day), with soap operas bubbling on the tube day and night, able to give vicarious thrills to 50 million fans at a time, acting like a drug, especially on children, who hypnotically learn commercials (Wynn, 1977).

Celebrities comprise a never-ending pantheon of popular fantasy figures—John Wayne, Elvis Presley, the Beatles, Michael Jackson, Boy George, Jackie Onassis, Liz Taylor, Frank Sinatra, Marilyn Monroe, Rudolf Valentino. Their presentation is not only a show but a cult, if one considers behavior of devotees, called fans, who follow their idol wherever he appears, to applaud and collect his pictures, autographs, and relics (Klapp, 1949; 1964; 1969:239–255). Celebrities provide not only fantasy roles in media as already observed, but their own rise to wealth and fame is a wonderful success story with Cinderella's magic, whose message is, "If they, why not I?" John Lahr (1978) has analyzed well what the "fame game" does for America. Its function is to keep alive the "democratic mythology of success," the "romance of individualism," in a nation of recent immigrants anxious to "assuage the trauma of being uprooted" by establishing a name. He sees the fame game as a compensatory mechanism legitimizing American institutions:

Winners in a competitive society, stars of free enterprise, the famous are flaunted so that the system can be seen to work. . . . These displays . . . create a sense of well-being and possibility. They make American life seem a blessing. . . . America's dream has always been more important to it than its reality, and the famous are living proof of the dream. As the society flounders without a lofty mission and with its institutions in disarray, the machinery of celebrity works even harder to produce a sense of the culture's greatness. Celebrity proliferates in proportion to the society's fear of its decay (Lahr, 1978).

But in other countries, Italians, Frenchmen, Indians and Egyptians also idolize celebrities. As I see it, palliating the trauma of uprootedness is only one function of the cult of celebrities, which, in modern and modernizing countries the world over, consoles people for various ills of modern living—any ache that can be soothed by Cinderella's magic. Such a hospitable pantheon arouses hope and sustains faith in much the same way as does a lottery by its occasional sweepstakes winnings for a few lucky ones.

Another institution that is like a Christmas tree loaded with placebos is Disneyland/World, which seems to please everybody, both young and old, and as an attraction to foreign tourists outdraws even the Grand Canyon. There one can visit Cinderella's Castle and Magic Kingdom, or far-off regions of Adventureland, or Liberty Square to capture the spirit of colonial America. In this world of fantasy the Dwarfs come to life: one can also meet Mickey Mouse, Goofy, the Wizard of Oz, Alice in Wonderland, Sleeping Beauty, the Keystone Cops, and so on. Doubtless children delight at seeing storybook characters come to life, but to adults part of the appeal is plainly nostalgia, with a wish to give children the same experiences parents once had. There is also pride in technology, that America is a place where such wonders occur. One sees also the theme of the success story, inherent in Disney's own rise from cartoonist-creator of Mickey Mouse to head of a great enterprise. A former marketing director of Disneyland, Edwin Ettinger, attributed the enormous growth of this enterprise to its power to appease boredom of a generation with ever more leisure on their hands and not knowing quite what to do with it. He said: "It was a kind of mass groping. . . . They felt awkward about all that leisure time thrust onto them and they weren't sure what to do with it. Sure, they had their two cars, their pool and their golf and all that—the great American dream. But they were still bored and they weren't sure why" (Los Angeles *Times*, July 12, 1970). Revealing is the explanation by Disneyland ambassador Raellen Lescault of the attraction of Main Street U.S.A.: It is "a place where dreams come true" (MacDonald, 1978). Disney himself is reported to have said, "It might not be what Main Street really was, always clean, always happy, always gay—but it is darn well what Main Street ought to be" (Waugh, 1972).

What it comes to, I think, is that Disney fantasy is not just romantic, unrealistic escape, but also a world in which part of the American dream is realized—a place where dreams come true if nowhere else. Make-believe fulfills pet notions, ingrained during childhood, which adults are delighted to see brought to life by artifice. No one objects to make-believe; rather there is eagerness for fun for kids and nostalgic reinforcement for their parents. Asserting the ideal, Disneyland is a sort of bonbon that consoles us for what may have been missing from the dinner.

This perception may help explain the mistrust that has arisen about such a benign institution. Critics (Schickel, 1968; Roszak, 1972:22–25; Real, 1977) have severely questioned it—which seems rather like knocking apple pie. But I think mistrust comes from perceiving that it is not merely a pleasant fairy tale but a placebo that fosters and works by false consciousness.

All these types of placebo—material consolations, chemical placebos, active outlets, and vicarious catharsis—work together in a battery to help ease tensions, so high in modern society. Do they really reduce tension? It is not necessary to assume that they do, for, by the metaphor of the leaky ship, the water in the hold may be rising as fast as the pumps work. Anyway, consolation and compensation do not have to imply tension reduction. Because of objection to the safety-valve idea that it is too mechanical and simplistic, I prefer the idea of placebo, whose consolation includes tension reduction but does not hinge on it.

The dimension of false consciousness becomes more important to the working of placebos as we de-emphasize tension reduction and stress the power of suggestion to console by making imaginary rewards real and prophecies fulfill themselves.

How do we know that institutions—courts, schools, churches, elections, penal systems, armies, armaments—really work, aside from our idea that they do? Seldom are laws or social programs scientifically tested before or after being enacted, as positivists (Lundberg, 1961) complain. In many cases, all we have going is the faith factor. Where that is the case, there is prudence in the saying, "Don't knock placebo, it may be all we have."

The problem of false consciousness arises wherever there is ideology, sustained by faith and loaded with promises of consolation and reward. Sociologists are indebted to Karl Mannheim (1936) who took Marx's ideas about ideology being a smokescreen for class interests, and generalized them into the more sweeping statement that modern society continually generates false consciousness in two main systematic forms: ideology preserving the present structure from change, and utopia as an unreal vision of the future. Mannheim wrote:

It was Marxist theory which first ... gave new emphasis to the role of class position and class interests in thought (p. 74). . . . As a result of the expansion of the ideological concept, a new mode of understanding has gradually come into existence (p. 76). . . . As long as one does not call his own position into question but regards it as absolute, while interpreting his opponent's ideas as a mere function of the social positions they occupy, the decisive step forward has not yet been taken.... [In the total conception of ideology] one subjects not just the adversary's point of view but all points of view, including his own, to the ideological analysis.... The thought of all parties in all epochs is of an ideological character (p. 77).... Beyond the commonly recognized sources of error we just also reckon with the effects of a distorted mental structure.... The reality to be comprehended is distorted and concealed (p. 97).... The unmasking of ideologies always takes the form of self-clarification for society as a whole (p. 262).

Unfortunately, though science has a mission to transcend ideology, it is not free from it. It has its own ideology, scientism (Whyte, 1956; Roszak, 1972). According to this view, false consciousness is unavoidable in our society, for all its information, and social placebos have some connection with it. The difficulty of analysis is that you can have false consciousness and not know it; indeed, its curious symptom is that the patient proclaims himself to be free of it—seeing things as they are. Ideology can help hide discrepancies that might be uncomfortable (such as that a so-called free market is really oligopoly, or a government calling itself a people's republic is really a tyranny, or that a church that burns heretics is anti-Christian, or that public service is really the profit of special interests). The main point is this: once we apply terms like ideology or myth to something others believe, we admit the existence of false consciousness of which the *subject is unaware*. Turnabout is fair play: it follows that we, too, are subject to false consciousness. If we all live in a hall of distorting mirrors, who may say he sees it as it is?

Thus, to speak of others' false consciousness is to be in a position like that of the detective in a murder mystery who is deductively certain that the murderer is in the house, but unable to prove which of a dozen suspects is guilty—or that all are.

What, then, is an intelligent position when false consciousness is accepted as a fact of life, our own no less than others'? Aware that one cannot tell which part of ideology is false (and abjuring a godlike claim to be able to), it seems reasonable to suspend faith toward all glittering generalities and refuse to take institutions at their face value, discounting them, just as a trader knows there are prices behind prices, discounts of discounts, veneers beneath veneers, and that a rare bargain sometimes turns out to be a common gyp. If Freud would not accept his patients' claims at face value, why should we do so with institutions that say, "We are serving you," "We are making you happy," "We are protecting you"? In other words, an intelligent position is to become aware of an inflation in values, in which ideology works like counterfeit money to make us feel richer than we really are.

Getting back to placebo institutions, then, what is their connection with false consciousness? It seems to me to be a working relationship, in which each helps the other. Institutions work as placebos to the degree to which they (1) are accepted in lieu of something better; (2) give consolation or relief, helping satisfy people with institutions that are not working all that well; (3) produce real benefits by faith, hope, or suggestion; and (4) work by and foster false consciousness. As examples of institutions having such functions, we mentioned carnivals, mockery, disco-dancing, gambling, lotteries, giveaway games, ads, sports spectacles, pinball arcades, alcohol and drugs, binges, saki parties, sentimental drama and fiction, Disneyland, and even political actions.

If one asks, how do placebo institutions help? two answers promptly suggest themselves. On the one hand, placebos provide consolation or relief. On the other hand, they can reduce awareness, hide discrepancies, act as a smokescreen, foster dreams and fantasies, put a better face on things, making us feel they are better than they actually are. Either way, such functions could help save institutions from a crisis of legitimacy (Habermas, 1975).

Then what is the role of placebo institutions in mass affluence? We note that affluent societies are loaded with placebos: a battery of arrangements that assuage and compensate for tensions while supporting a facade of happiness. Affluent societies are not only loaded with placebos but high in tensions, such as boredom and identity problems, that show no sign of declining. Indeed, the relationship of placebos to tension is probably better characterized as *direct* (the more placebos, the more tension) than *inverse* (the more placebos, the less tension) as one would expect if placebos were simply a remedy. Of course, it might be merely that water was coming into the ship's hold faster than pumps can draw it down.

But I think a more complex picture is needed: one that does not rule out simple tension reduction but stresses masking or *changing awareness* of tensions that may remain high (just as Freud said sublimation and rationalization do not eliminate tensions but make them look better to us). So drugs, gambling, sports spectacles, Harlequin romances, Disneyland, and so on could romanticize an existence as filled with tension as ever by putting a better face on it. Placebo institutions might console by changing awareness in such ways as taking people's minds off real troubles, reducing awareness of negative tensions, as does Novocain or aspirin; diverting attention from complex problems to butts and scapegoats; changing the meaning of deprivation from fault of a system to bad luck (gambling); taking giveaways as proof of prosperity for all (just as the Roman games proved the generosity of emperors); accepting environmental pollution as the price of progress; viewing high tension and stress diseases as a mark of success (the stomach ulcer a "wound stripe of civilization"); fostering dreams and myths (celebrity success story, crime does not pay, Harlequin romance); not to leave out the real benefits from the self-fulfilling prophecy: expectations working by faith, hope, or suggestion. With enough placebo institutions, tension might be as strong as ever, but like a rose by another name smell sweeter.

A notable example of how placebos put a better face on things is leaders, corporations, media and education continually proclaiming the doctrine of progress. As the historian J.B. Bury (1921) pointed out, such an optimistic faith (that happiness and well-being continually increase with knowledge and affluence) is not a fact of nature, like evolution, but a dogma. As part of the modern ideology (shared by communists and capitalists, I might add), it makes us more contented with "growth" than otherwise we might be. In its most grossly ideological form it is merely a euphemistic label put on things that might be otherwise named as environmental damage, multinational corporate profits, colonial exploitation, diseconomies of scale (Kohr, 1977; Schumacher, 1973), or ethnocide (Bodley, 1974).

In short, I would argue that it is with placebo institutions as with doctors' pink pills: if doctors are prescribing more pink pills than ever, this tells us not that more ailments are being cured but that there are more needing relief. Tensions and placebos go hand in hand. Because placebos are consolatory and compensatory rather than remedial, one may expect that the more aspirin sold, the more headaches are being suffered. Likewise, the more Harlequin romances, the more unhappy marriages; the more law enforcement, the more crime; the more bloody sports spectacles, the more rioting at sports events and violence in the streets. The proliferation of pleasure institutions in modern society could mean growth of the very tensions for which placebos are needed. All the same, patients are more consoled with placebos than without them.

Are placebos good? I suppose it comes down to whether you like the institution that is shielded by them. Evaluation depends on what they are used for. Medically, they are justified if, in absence of more effective treatment, they bring comfort or help an effective treatment to give even better results. A little faith in a pink pill seems a small price to pay for real relief. Likewise for society, placebos have a place where effective measures are lacking, or they help a useful program or institution to work even better, perhaps by converting hope into morale. It is another matter if false consciousness produced by placebos stands in the way of improving an institution, even protects a bad one. The case for social placebos seems the same as for medical: at best they make life a little easier for people; at worse they impede remedy and may themselves become a problem (as in the case of addiction). So the faith factor works in uneasy partnership with the fake factor, justifying white lies for the patient's good.

It might be better if placebos infallibly reduced tension and we were all comfortably sedated and swaddled. But, because the meaning sustained by placebos is to some extent spurious, there is continual leakage of negative tension around and in spite of their consolations (such as perceiving "success" as a rat race, "progress" as pollution). Perhaps never before the 1960s has an educated generation been so aware that its mentality was restricted by the life style of affluence; the drop-out and consciousness-expansion movements proved that. Mistrust of images—awareness of hype, hokum, and fake—is a large part of the tension of modern man. It is safe to say that because of such leakage, critics will prick balloons of comfort, ungratefully finding fault with the "consciousness industry" of media, "happy consciousness" of supermarket society, Disneyland, and so on, without either critics or defenders being able to prove they are right.

We have here looked at some factors—material consolations, chemical placebos, activity outlets, and vicarious consolations—that play some part in assuaging tensions such as boredom and frustration that arise in a society loaded with noiselike information and banality, and short on meaning, as described. However, they do not remedy sources of tension but merely make people feel better about an unsatisfactory state of affairs. So they relieve tensions that otherwise might threaten the stability of the system. Social placebos can help avert a meaning crisis. Just as hypnosis can tell a patient that his pain is not there, so, false consciousness, engendered in part by placebos, can tell a society that a problem such as boredom or meaning crisis is not there. Suggestion is such a powerful force it could easily make invisible a much larger problem than boredom. So, I venture, a cocoon of comfort created by placebos helps assuage the irritation of noise and the mind-numbing impact of banality.

BIBLIOGRAPHY

Abramson, Edward E.; and Stinson, Shaun G. "Boredom and Eating in Obese and Non-obese Individuals," *Addictive Behaviors* 2 (1977): 181–85.

Allen, Frederick Lewis. *Only Yesterday*. New York: Harper and Brothers, 1931.

Allport, Gordon; and Postman, Leo. *Psychology of Rumor*, New York: Henry Holt, 1947.

Andrews, Frank M.; and Withey, Stephen B. *Social Indicators of Well-Being*. New York: Plenum Publishing Corp., 1976.

Ashby, W. Ross. *An Introduction to Cybernetics*. London: Methuen and Co., Ltd., 1956.

Asheim, Lester. "Ortega Revisited," *Library Quarterly* 52 (July 1982): 215–26.

Babcock, Barbara A., ed. *The Reversible World*. Ithaca: Cornell University Press, 1978.

Bateson, Gregory. *Steps to an Ecology of Mind*. New York: Ballantine Books, 1972.

Becker, Ernest. *The Birth and Death of Human Meaning*. New York: Free Press, 1962.

Beckett, Samuel. *The Lost Ones*. New York: Grove Press, 1972.

Beer, Stafford. *The Brain of the Firm*. New York: McGraw-Hill, 1972.

Belloc, Hilaire. "A Guide to Boring," in *A Conversation with a Cat*. New York: Harper & Bros., 1931.

Berlyne, D. E. *Conflict, Arousal and Curiosity*. New York: McGraw-Hill, 1960.

Berlyne, D.E.; and Madsen, K.B., eds. *Pleasure, Reward, Preference*. New York: Academic Press, 1973.

————. *Structure and Direction in Thinking*, New York: John Wiley & Sons, 1965.

————. ed. *Studies in the New Experimental Aesthetics*. Washington, D.C.: Hemisphere Publishing Corp., 1974.

Bernays, Anne. *Growing Up Rich*. Boston: Little, Brown and Co., 1975.

Bernstein, Haskel E. "Boredom and the Ready-Made Life," *Social Research* 42 (Autumn 1975): 512–37.

Bettelheim, Bruno. *The Uses of Enchantment*. New York: A. A. Knopf, 1976.

Birdwhistell, Ray L. *Kinesics and Context*. New York: Ballantine Books, 1970.

Bishop, Jerry E. "Potent Non-Drugs, Placebos," *Wall Street Journal*, August 25, 1977, pp. 1, 21.

Blau, Peter M. *Bureaucracy in Modern Society*. New York: Random House, 1956.

Blumenthal, Albert. *Small Town Stuff*. Chicago: University of Chicago Press, 1932.

Bodley, John H. *Victims of Progress*. New York: Addison-Wesley, 1974.

Boorstin, Daniel J. *The Image, or What happened to the American Dream*. New York: Atheneum, 1962.

Boulding, Kenneth. *Ecodynamics: A New Theory of Societal Evolution*, Beverly Hills, Calif.: Sage Publications, 1978.

Brown, Curtis F. *Star-Spangled Kitsch*. New York: Universe Books, 1975.

Brunner, Ronald D., and Chen, Kan. "Is Cable the Answer?" *Journal of Communication* 28 (Spring 1978), 81–84.

Buchsbaum, Monte S. "Tuning in on Hemispheric Dialogue," *Psychology Today*, January 1979, p. 100.

Budzinski, Thomas H. "Tuning in on the Twilight Zone," *Psychologq Today*, August 1977, pp. 38–44.

Bury, J. B. *The Idea of Progress*. New York: Macmillan Co., 1932 (first published 1921).

Campbell, Angus. *The Sense of Well-Being in America*. New York: McGraw-Hill Book Company, 1981.

————; Converse, Philip E.; and Rodgers, Willard L. *The Quality of American Life*. New York: Russell Sage Foundation, 1976.

Campbell, Felicia. "The Future of Gambling," *The Futurist*, April 1976, pp. 84–90.

Carey, James W. "The Communications Revolution and the Professional Communicator," *Sociological Review Monographs*, January 1969, pp. 23–38.

Carmel, Jeffrey J. "What's Behind the Rebellion of Swiss Youth?" *Christian Science Monitor*, October 28, 1980, p. 8.

Carter, Richard F.; Pyska, Ronald H.; and Guerraro, Jose L. "Dissonance and Exposure to Aversive Information," *Journalism Quarterly*, Spring, 1969, pp. 37–42.

Cavett, Dick. "Dick Cavett Show," Public Broadcasting System, March 1, 1979.

Chapin, F. Stuart. *Cultural Change*, New York: The Century Co., 1928.

————. "A Theory of Synchronous Culture Cycles," *Journal of Social Forces*, May 1924.

Christian, William A., Jr. *Person and God in a Spanish Village*. New York: Seminar Press, 1972.

Colby, Benjamin N. "Behavioral Redundancy," *Behavioral Science* 3 (1958): 317–22.

Colligan, Michael J.; and Stockton, William. "The Mystery of Assembly-Line Hysteria," *Psychology Today*, June 1978, pp. 93–94.

Compaine, Benjamin M. "The Magazine Industry: Developing the Special Interest Audience," *Journal of Communication* 30 (Spring 1980): 98–103.

Cooley, Charles H. *Social Organization*. New York: Charles Scribner's Sons, 1927 (originally published 1909).

Cooper, Kip. "Officers, Top Enlisted Personnel Warned of Immediate Discharge," *San Diego Union*, December 10, 1981.

Cornish, Edward, ed. *Communications Tomorrow*. Bethesda, Md.: The World Future Society, 1982.

Coser, Lewis A. *Functions of Social Conflict*. Glencoe, Ill.: Free Press, 1956.

Cousins, Norman. "The Mysterious Placebo," *Saturday Review*, October 1, 1977, pp. 9–16.

Cowley, Deborah. "The Last Nomad," *Christian Science Monitor*, May 22, 1980, p. 15.

Crain, Robert L.; Katz, Elihu; and Rosenthal, Donald B. *The Politics of Community Conflict*, Indianapolis, Ind.: Bobbs-Merrill, 1969.

Critchfield, Richard. "Youths Tune Out Dogma," *Christian Science Monitor*, August 1, 1980.

Csikszentmihalyi, Mihaly. *Beyond Boredom and Anxiety*. San Francisco: Jossey-Bass Publishers, 1975.

Davies, Hunter. "The Beatles," *Life*, September 20, 1968, p. 62.

Davis, Fred. *Yearning for Yesterday*. New York: Free Press, 1979.

Deeley, Peter. "Australia's Battle with Alcoholism," *Christian Science Monitor*, Janaury 9, 1978.

Deutsch, Karl W. *The Nerves of Government*. New York: Free Press, 1966.

———. "On Social Communication and the Metropolis," *Daedalus* 90 (1961): 99–110.

Dixon, Norman F. *Subliminal Perception*. London: McGraw-Hill, 1971.

Dizard, Wilson. *The Coming Information Age*. New York: Longman, Inc., 1982.

Dominick, Joseph R.; and Pearce, Millard C. "Trends in Prime-Time Programming," *Journal of Communication* 26 (Winter 1976): 77.

Dorfles, Gillo. *Kitsch, the World of Bad Taste*. New York: Universe Books, 1969.

Dowell, William. "Fighting Alcohol in France," *Christian Science Monitor*, July 29, 1980, pp. 1, 18.

Durkheim, Emile. *The Division of Labor in Society*. Glencoe, Ill.: The Free Press, 1947 (originally published 1893).

Easwaran, Eknath. *Gandhi the Man*, Berkeley, Calif.: Nilgiri Press, 1978.

Ehrenzweig, Anton. *The Hidden Order in Art*. London: Palladin, 1970.

Ellul, Jacques. *The Technological Society*. New York: A. A. Knopf, 1965.

Evans-Pritchard, E. E. *Witchcraft, Ordeals and Magic Among the Azande*. Oxford: Clarendon Press, 1937.

Fenwick, Henry. "The Many Ways to a Beautiful Face," *San Francisco Chronicle*, April 26, 1979, p. 24.

Ferguson, Marilyn. *The Aquarian Conspiracy*. Los Angeles: J. P. Tarcher, 1980.

Ferris, Charles. Quoted by Louise Sweeney, *Christian Science Monitor*, January 26, 1978, p. 26.

Festinger, Leon. *A Theory of Cognitive Dissonance*, Evanston, Ill.: Row, Peterson, 1957.

————; Riecken, H. W.; and Schachter, Stanley. *When Prophecy Fails*. Minneapolis: University of Minnesota Press, 1956.

Fiske, Edward B. "The Selling of the Deity," *Saturday Review*, December 9, 1972, pp. 17–18.

Forbes-Boyd, Eric. "The Year of the Ragwort," *Christian Science Monitor*, Janaury 18, 1978.

Fortune, Reo. *Sorcerers of Dobu*. London: G. Routledge and Sons, 1932.

Fowler, H. W. *A Dictionary of Modern English Usage*, Oxford: Clarendon Press, 1974.

Frankl, Victor E. *The Unheard Cry for Meaning*, New York: Simon & Schuster, 1978.

Freedman, Jonathan L.; and Sears, David O. "Selective Exposure," in Leonard Berkowitz, ed., *Advances in Experimental Social Psychology*, vol. 2. New York: Academic Press, 1965, pp. 57–97.

Gallup, George H. "What Mankind Thinks About Itself," *Reader's Digest*, October 1976, pp. 25–31.

Garland, Hamlin. *Boy Life on the Prairie*, New York: Washington Square Press, 1965 (originally published 1899).

Garson, Barbara. *All the Livelong Day, the Meaning and Demeaning of Routine Work*. New York: Penguin Books, 1975.

Georgescu-Roegen, Nicholas. *The Entropy Law and the Economic Process*. Cambridge, Mass.: Harvard University Press, 1971.

Gilchrist, J.; Shaw, M.; and Walker, L. "Some Effects of Unequal Distribution of Information in a Wheel Group Structure," *Journal of Abnormal and Social Psychology* 51 (1955): 119–22.

Gluckman, Max. *Custom and Conflict in Africa*. Glencoe, Ill.: The Free Press, 1965.

Goblot, Edmund. "Cultural Education as a Middle-Class Enclave," in Elizabeth and Tom Burns, eds., *Sociology, Literature and Drama*. Harmondsworth, Middlesex, England: Penguin Books, 1973, pp. 433–44.

Gombrich, E. H. *The Sense of Order*. Oxford: Phaidon Press, Ltd., 1979.

Goodwin, James. Report in *Brain-Mind Bulletin* 4 (August 6, 1979): 3.

Gorz, Andre. *Strategy for Labor*. Boston: Beacon Press, 1967.

Gotlieb, Allan E.; and Gwynn, Richard J. "Social Planning of Communication," in B. Singer, ed., *Communications in Canadian Society*. Toronto: Copp Clark Publishing Co., 1972, pp. 86–97.

Granzberg, Gary. "Television as Storyteller: The Algonkian Indians of Central Canada," *Journal of Communication* 32 (Winter 1982): 43–52.

Graham, Victoria. "The Myth and Memory of Elvis," *San Diego Union*, August 13, 1978.

Greenberg, Peter F. "The Thrill Seekers," *Human Behavior* 6 (April 1977): 16–21.

Greiff, Constance M., ed. *Lost America*. Princeton, N.J.: Pyne Press, 1971.

Habermas, Jurgen. *Legitimation Crisis*. Boston: Beacon Press, 1975.

Harary, Frank; and Batell, Mark F. "The Concept of Negative Information," *Behavior Science* 23 (July 1978): 264–70.

Hardy, Thomas. *Far from the Madding Crowd*, London: Macmillan London Ltd., 1974 (first published 1874).

Harlow, Harry F. "The Heterosexual Affectional System in Monkeys," in Warren G. Bennis et al., eds., *Interpersonal Dynamics*. Homewood, Ill.: Dorsey Press, 1968, pp. 43–60.

Hart, Hornell. "Logistic Social Trends," *American Journal of Sociology*, March 1945, pp. 337–52.

Heidegger, Martin. *Discourse on Thinking*. New York: Harper & Row, 1966.

Henderson, Hazel. *Creating Alternate Futures*. New York: G. P. Putnam's Sons, 1978.

Heron, Woodburn. "The Pathology of Boredom," *Scientific American* 196 (January 1957): 52–56.

Herzog, Arthur. *The B. S. Factor*. New York: Simon & Schuster, 1973.

Hiltz, Starr Roxanne; and Turoff, Murray. *The Network Nation: Human Communication via Computer*. New York: Addison-Wesley Publ. Co., 1978.

Hirschi, Travis. *Causes of Delinquency*. Berkeley: University of California Press, 1969.

Hirschman, Albert O. *Shifting Involvements*. Princeton, N.J.: Princeton University Press, 1982.

Hoffer, Eric. *The True Believer*. New York: Harper, 1951.

Horn, Jack. "Bored to Sickness," *Psychology Today*, November 1975, p. 92.

Hughes, Robert. "The World of Steinberg," *Time*, April 17, 1978, p. 64.

Hurwitz, Sol. "The Corporate Role," *Journal of Communication* 28 (Spring 1978): 73–76.

Hutshing, Ed. "Book Beat," *San Diego Union*, January 20, 1985.

Huxley, Aldous. *Brave New World*. Garden City, N.Y.: Doubleday, Doran & Co., 1932.

Ionesco, Eugene. "Ionesco on Politics," *Los Angeles Times*, May 18, 1980.

Jacklin, Phil. "Representative Diversity," *Journal of Communication* 28 (Spring 1978): 85–88.

James, William. *On Some of Life's Ideals*. New York: Henry Holt & Co., 1899.
———. *Memories and Studies*. London: Longmans, Green & Co., 1911.

Janis, Irving L. *Victims of Groupthink*, Boston: Houghton Mifflin Co., 1972.

Jennings, Lane. "The Human Side of Tomorrow's Communications," *The Futurist*, April 1979, pp. 104–8.

Jenson, Gregory. "World's Greatest Tourist Sites Slamming the Doors on Visitors," *UPI, London Free Press* (Ontario), February 17, 1979.

Johnson, Weldon T. "The Religious Crusade," *American Journal of Sociology* 76 (1971): 875–90.

Jones, Clayton. "Quiet Rural Town . . . Smoking Pot," *Christian Science Monitor*, July 6, 1978.

Kaplan, H. Roy. "The Convergence of Work, Sport and Gambling in America," *Annals of the American Academy of Political and Social Science* 445 (September 1979): 24–38.

Kaplan, Robert, et al. *Job Demands and Worker Health*. Washington, D.C.: U.S. Government Printing Office, 1975.

Katz, Elihu. "Can Authentic Cultures Survive New Media?" *Journal of Communication* 27 (Spring 1977): 113–21.

Key, Wilson Bryan. *Subliminal Seduction*. Englewood Cliffs, N.J.: Prentice-Hall, Inc., 1973.

Kishida, Koya. "Temporal Change of Subsidiary Behavior in Monotonous Work," *Journal of Human Ergology* 2 (September 1973): 75–89.

Klapp, Orrin E. *Collective Search for Identity*. New York: Holt, Rinehart and Winston, 1969.

————. "Hero Worship in America," *American Sociological Review*, 14 (February 1949): 53–62.

————. *Opening and Closing*. New York: Cambridge University Press, 1978.

————. *Symbolic Leaders, Public Dramas and Public Men*, Chicago, Ill.: Aldine Publishing Co., 1964.

Kohr, Leopold. *The Overdeveloped Nations*. New York: Schocken Books, 1977.

Kostelanetz, Richard, ed. *Seeing Through Shuck*. New York: Ballantine Books, 1972.

Kraus, J. "Causes of Delinquency as Perceived by Juveniles," *International Journal of Offender Therapy and Comparative Criminology* 21 (1977): 79–86.

Kroger, William S. *Clinical and Experimental Hypnosis*. Philadelphia: J. B. Lippincott Co., 1963.

Krutsch, Joseph Wood. *The Measure of Man*, Indianapolis, Ind.: Bobbs-Merrill, 1954.

Kucera, Henry; and Francis, W. Nelson. *Computational Analysis of Present-Day American English*. Providence, R.I.: Brown University Press, 1967.

Kuhn, Reinhard Clifford. *The Demon of Noontide*. Princeton, N.J.: Princeton University Press, 1976.

Lahr, John. "The Fame Game," *Los Angeles Times*, January 1, 1978 (copyright by Harper's Magazine Co., 1977).

Lanternari, Vittorio. *Religions of the Oppressed*. New York: Knopf, Mentor, 1963.

Larkin, Ralph W. *Suburban Youth in Cultural Crisis*. New York: Oxford University Press, 1979.

Leontief, Wassily. "A Nobel Winner's Remedy..." *Christian Science Monitor*, August 27, 1982, p. 23.

Lerner, Daniel. *The Passing of Traditional Society*. New York: The Free Press, 1958.

Levine, Grace Ferrari. "Learned Helplessness and the Evening News," *Journal of Communication* 27 (Autumn 1977): 100–105.

Levine, Jo Ann. "Romance—a Literary Trend," *Christian Science Monitor*, September 13, 1977.

Levy, Mark R.; and Fink, Edward L. "Home Video Recorders and the Transiency of Television Broadcasts," *Journal of Communication* 34 (Spring 1984): 56–71.

Lewis, I. M. *Ecstatic Religion*. Harmondsworth, Middlesex, England: Penguin Books, Ltd., 1971.

Linder, Staffan Burenstam. *The Harried Leisure Class*. New York: Columbia University Press, 1970.

Linton, Thomas E.; and Pollack, Erwin W. "Boredom Transcended: Adolescent Survival in the Suburban Highschool," *High School Journal* 62 (November 1978): 69–72.

Lippman, Walter. *Public Opinion*. New York: Harcourt Brace & Co., 1922.

Litman, Barry R. "Is Network Ownership in the Public Interest?" *Journal of Communication* 28 (Spring 1978): 51–59.

Loercher, Diana. "Book Publishing Has Become Bigger," *Christian Science Monitor*, June 2, 1978.

———. "Margaret Mead Pleads for Vanishing Peoples," *Christian Science Monitor*, October 26, 1977, p. 29.

Lomax, Alan. "Appeal for Cultural Equity," *Journal of Communication* 27 (Spring 1977): 125–38.

Lull, James. "Popular Music: Resistance to New Wave," *Journal of Communication* 32 (Winter 1982): 121–31.

Lundberg, George H. *Can Science Save Us?* New York: Longmans, Green and Co., revised edition, 1961.

MacCannel, Dean. "Staged Authenticity: Arrangements of Social Space in Tourist Settings," *American Journal of Sociology* 79 (November 1973): 589–603.

———. *The Tourist*. New York: Schocken Books, 1976.

MacDonald, Craig. "She's bound by Disney's Spell," *San Diego Union*, February 17, 1978.

Macdonald, Dwight. "A Theory of Mass Culture," in B. Rosenberg and D. White, eds., *Mass Culture*. New York: Free Press, 1957.

Machlup, Fritz. *Knowledge and Knowledge Production*, vol. 1. Princeton, N.J.: Princeton University Press, 1980.

MacKay, Donald M. *Information, Mechanism, and Meaning*, Cambridge, Mass.: M.I.T. Press, 1969.

————; and McCulloch, W. W. "The Limiting Information Capacity of a Neural Link," *Bulletin of Mathematical Biophysics* 14 (1952): 127–35.

Maddocks, Melvin. "How to Speak Without an Accent," *Christian Science Monitor*, January 25, 1979.

————. "Is Journalism a Bowl of Spinach in a Candy Factory?" *Christian Science Monitor*, December 28, 1978, p. 22.

Mannheim, Karl. *Ideology and Utopia.* New York: Harcourt Brace & Co., 1936.

Manning, Robert. "International News Media," in Arthur S. Hoffman, ed., *International Communication and the New Diplomacy.* Bloomington: Indiana University Press, 1968.

Marcuse, Herbert. *One-Dimensional Man.* London: Routledge and Kegan Paul, Ltd., 1964.

Marlin, William. "Finding Form in the Human Equation," *Christian Science Monitor*, September 15, 1977.

Martin, Christopher. *The Bored Electors.* London: Darton, Longman and Todd, 1961.

Maslow, Abraham. *Toward a Psychology of Being*, New York: D. Van Nostrand Co., 1962.

————. *Farther Reaches of Human Nature*, New York: Viking, 1971.

Masuda, Yoneji. *The Information Society as Post-Industrial Society.* Bethesda, Md.: The World Future Society, 1981.

McHugh, Peter. *Defining the Situation.* Indianapolis, Ind.: Bobbs-Merrill Co., 1968.

McLuhan, Marshall. Preface to Robert Wallis, *Time: Fourth Dimension of the Mind.* New York: Harcourt, Brace & World, 1968, p. vii.

Meerloo, Joost A. M. In Frank E. X. Dance, ed., *Human Communication Theory*, New York: Holt, Rinehart & Winston, 1967, p. 133.

Meier, Richard L. *A Communications Theory of Urban Growth.* Cambridge, Mass.: Joint Center for Urban Studies of M.I.T. and Harvard University, M.I.T. Press, 1962.

————. "Communications Stress," *Annual Review of Ecology and Systematics* 3 (1972): 289–314.

Merton, Robert K. *Social Theory and Social Structure.* Glencoe, Ill.: The Free Press, 1949.

————. *Social Theory and Social Structure*, New York: Free Press, 1968.

Meyer, Karl E. "The Gaming of America," *Saturday Review*, October 28, 1978, p. 37.

Mill, John Stuart. *On Liberty.* 1859.

Miller, George A. *Psychology of Communication.* New York: Basic Books, 1967.

Miller, James Grier. "Information Input Overload and Psychopathology," *American Journal of Psychiatry* 116 (February 1960): 695–704.

Mitchell, J. Clyde, ed. *Social Networks in Urban Situations.* Manchester: University of Manchester Press, 1969.

Morgan, Judith. "Boring in on Excitement, British-Style," *San Diego Union*, December 20, 1981.

Mortimer, John. "Raquel: the thoughts of a detached sex symbol," *The Sunday Times*, London, England, October 28, 1984, p. 10.

Murray, Geoffrey. "Japanese Become World's Great Adventurers," *Christian Science Monitor*, June 4, 1980, p. 2.

Myers, Gordon. *The Sinking Ark*. New York: Pergamon, 1979.

Nelson, Joyce. "TV Formulas: Prime Time Glue," *In Search/En Quĕte*, Fall 1979, p. 18.

Nemy, Enid. "We Wouldn't Want to Bore You, But..." New York Times News Service, *San Diego Union*, Febraury 3, 1980.

Nevin, Margaret. "Rachel Zylberberg Makes Good," *Weekend Magazine, Globe and Mail*, January 27, 1979, pp. 4–5.

Nicolis, G.; and Prigogine, I. *Self-Organization in Nonequilibrium Systems*. New York: John Wiley & Sons, 1977.

Norton, Clark. "Will PAC-MAN End Western Civilization?" *Inquiry*, May 17, 1982, pp. 18–20.

Ogburn, William F. *Social Change*. New York: B. W. Huebsch, 1922.

Omang, Joanne. "Norman Rockwell," *San Diego Union*, March 23, 1969.

Ortega y Gasset, Jose. *The Revolt of the Masses*. New York: W. W. Norton & Co., 1932.

Orwell, George. *1984, a Novel*. New York: Harcourt, Brace, 1949.

Owens, David. "Inside Twentieth Century Music," *Christian Science Monitor*, January 14, 1982.

Packard, Vance. *The Hidden Persuaders*. New York: David McKay, 1957.

Palmer, Stuart. *Role Stress*. Englewood Cliffs, N.J.: Prentice-Hall, Inc., 1981.

Parsons, Talcott. *The Social System*. Glencoe, Ill.: Free Press, 1951.

Pascal, Blaise. *Pascal's Pensees*. New York: E. P. Dutton & Co., 1958.

Patterson, Blake. "Musical Dynamics," *Scientific American* 231 (November 1974): 78–95.

Pendse, Shripard. "Category Perception, Language and Brain Hemispheres," *Behavioral Science*, 23 (November 1978): 421–28.

Penfield, Wilder. "Memory Mechanisms," *A.M.A. Archives of Neurology and Psychiatry* 67 (1952): 178–98.

Peters, Edward. "Notes Toward an Archaeology of Boredom," *Social Research* 42 (Autumn 1975): 493–511.

Pierce, John R. *Symbols, Signals and Noise*. New York: Harper and Row, 1961.

Pool, Ithiel de Sola. "Direct Broadcast Satellites and the Integrity of National Cultures," in *Control of the Direct Broadcast Satellite*. Palo Alto, Calif.: Aspen Institute, an occasional paper, 1974, pp. 27–56.

Pope, Liston. *Millhands and Preachers*. New Haven, Conn.: Yale University Press, 1942.

Porat, Marc Uri. *The Information Economy: Definition and Measurement.* Washington, D.C.: U.S. Government Printing Office, July 1977.

―――. "Global Implications of the Information Society," *Journal of Communication* 28 (1978): 70–80.

Powdermaker, Hortense. *Hollywood the Dream Factory.* Boston: Little, Brown & Co., 1951.

Prasinos, Laraine. "Squealing Bat Boppers Run Wild in Greek Town," *Christian Science Monitor,* February 7, 1978.

Prescott, James. " 'Touching,' an Interview with Barbara Boynton," *Intellectual Digest,* March 1974, pp. 6–10.

Pund, Ernest E. "War Games Played Near Border," *San Diego Weekly News,* January 16, 1985.

Pye, Lucian W., ed. *Communications and Political Development.* Princeton, N.J.: Princeton University Press, 1963.

Quastler, H.; and Wulff, V. J. "Human Performance in Information Transmission," Control System Laboratory Report R–62. Urbana: University of Illinois, 1955.

Quinn, Robert P.; and Staines, Graham L. *The 1977 Quality of Employment Survey.* Ann Arbor: Survey Research Center, University of Michigan, 1978.

Rajneesh, Bhagwan Shree. *Meditation.* New York: Harper & Row, 1976.

Rapoport, Anatol, ed. *General Systems, Yearbook of the Society for General Systems Research* 21 (1976): p. v, editor's preface.

―――; and Kantor, R. E. "Complexity and Ambiguity in Environmental Design," *Journal American Institute of Planners,* July 1967.

Real, Michael R. *Mass-Mediated Culture.* Englewood Cliffs, N.Y.: Prentice-Hall, Inc., 1977.

Reasoner, Harry. "The Blanding of Tradition," *Christian Science Monitor,* December 19, 1974.

Renoir, Jean. *My Life and My Films,* New York: Atheneum Publishers, 1974.

Rifkin, Jeremy. *Entropy.* New York: Viking, 1980.

Robinson, Michael; and Olszewski, Ray. "Books in the Marketplace of Ideas," *Journal of Communication* 30 (Spring 1980): 81–88.

Rodin, Judith. "Causes and Consequences of Time Perception Differences in Overweight and Normal Weight People," *Journal of Personality and Social Psychology* 31 (1975): 898–910.

Rosnow, Ralph L.; and Fine, G. A. *Rumor and Gossip.* New York: Elsevier, 1976.

Roszak, Theodore. *Where the Wasteland Ends.* Garden City, N.Y.: Doubleday and Co., 1972.

Rothenbuler, Eric W.; and Dimmick, John W. "Popular Music: Concentration and Diversity in the Industry," *Journal of Communication* 32 (Winter 1982): 143–49.

Saranovic, Mihailo. "A Nonaligned View," *Christian Science Monitor,* October 25, 1978.

Sargent, William. *The Mind Possessed*, New York: Penguin Books, 1973.

Scheff, Thomas J. *Catharsis in Healing, Ritual and Drama*. Berkeley: University of California Press, 1980.

Schickel, Richard. *The Disney Version*. New York: Avon Books, Simon & Schuster, 1968.

Schiller, Herbert. *The Mind-Managers*. Boston: Beacon Press, 1973.

Schramm, Wilbur. *Men, Messages and Media, A Look at Human Communication*. New York: Harper and Row, Publishers, 1973.

Schrank, Jeffrey. *Snap, Crackle and Popular Taste*. New York: Dell, 1977.

Schubert, Daniel S. "Creativity and Coping With Boredom," *Psychiatric Annals* 8 (March 1978): 46–54.

Schumacher, E. F. *Small Is Beautiful*. New York: Harper and Row, 1973.

Schwartz, Gary; Turner, Paul; and Peluso, Emil. "Neither Heads nor Freaks: Working Class Drug Culture," *Urban Life and Culture* 2 (October 1973): 288–313.

Scitovsky, Tebor. *The Joyless Economy*. New York: Oxford University Press, 1976.

Seeman, Melvin. "Alienation in Pre-Crisis France," *American Sociological Review* 37 (August 1972): 385–402.

Shannon, Claude E.; and Weaver, Warren. *The Mathematical Theory of Communication*. Urbana: University of Illinois Press, 1949.

Shearer, Lloyd. "The Biggest Box Office Draw of All Time," *Parade*, December 18, 1966, p. 4.

Shibutani, Tamotsu. *Improvised News*. Indianapolis, Ind.: Bobbs-Merrill, 1966.

Shostrom, Everett L. *Man, the Manipulator*. New York: Abingdon, 1967; Bantam, 1968.

Siassi, Iradj; Crocetti, Guido and Spiro; and Herzl, R. "Loneliness and Dissatisfaction in a Blue Collar Population," *Archives of General Psychology*, 30 (February 1974): 261–65.

Silberman, Charles E. *Crisis in the Classroom*. New York: Random House, 1970.

Simmel, Georg. "Fashion," *American Journal of Sociology* 62 (1957): 541–58.

———. *The Sociology of Georg Simmel*. Glencoe, Ill.: The Free Press, 1950.

Simmons, William W. "The Consensor," *The Futurist*, April 1979, pp. 91–94.

Smith, Adam. "The Benefits of Boredom," *Psychology Today*, April 1976, pp. 46–51.

Smith, Richard P. "Boredom: A Review," *Human Factors* 23 (June 1981): 329–40.

Sobel, Robert. *The Manipulators*. New York: Anchor Press/Doubleday, 1976.

Sommer, Robert. *Personal Space*. Englewood Cliffs, N.J.: Prentice-Hall, Inc., 1969.

Sorokin, Pitirim. *The Crisis of Our Age*. New York: E.P. Dutton, 1941.

Stanford, Neal. "Flood of Scientific Data Rises," *Christian Science Monitor*, January 23, 1971.

Sternberg, Jacques. *Kitsch*. New York: St. Martin's, Press, 1971.

Sterritt, David. "Artists and Their Inspiration, Composer Steve Reich," *Christian Science Monitor*, October 23, 1980, p. 20.

Suedfeld, Peter. "The Benefits of Boredom: Sensory Deprivation Revisited," *American Scientist* 63 (Janaury-February 1975): 60–69.

Szulc, Tad. "Is Congress Obsolete?" *Saturday Review*, March 3, 1979, pp. 20–23.

Tec, Nechama. *Gambling in Sweden*. Totowa, N.J.: Bedminster Press, 1964.

Terkel, Studs. *Working*. New York: Pantheon Books, 1973.

Thorndike, Edward L.; and Lorge, Irving. *The Teacher's Word Book of 30,000 Words*. New York: Teachers College Press, Columbia University, 1944.

Toffler, Alvin. *Future Shock*. New York: Random House, 1970.

————. *The Third Wave*. New York: William Morrow & Co., 1980.

Townsend, Ed. "Drugs Bite at Business," *Christian Science Monitor*, August 5, 1970.

Toynbee, Arnold J. *A Study of History*. New York: Oxford University Press, 1947.

Tunstall, Jeremy. *The Media Are American*. New York: Columbia University Press, 1977.

Turner, Victor W. *The Ritual Process*. Chicago, Ill.: Aldine Publishing Co., 1969.

Van Gigue, John P. "The Physical and Mental Load Components of Objective Complexity in Production Systems," *Behavioral Science* 21 (1976): 490–97.

Veevers, Jean. *Childless by Choice*. Toronto: Butterworths, 1980.

Vinocur, John. "Vacationers Now Avoid Brighton," New York Times News Service, *San Diego Union*, August 17, 1979.

Wainman, Gord. "The Hard Way," *London Free Press* (Ontario), September 22, 1978.

Walker, Edward Lewis. "Complexity and Preference Theory," in D. Berlyne and K. B. Madsen, eds., *Pleasure, Reward, Preference*. New York: Academic Press, 1973.

Wallace, Robert. "The Rugged Basis of American Protestantism," *Life*, December 25, 1955, pp. 71.

Wangh, Martin. "Boredom in Psychoanalytic Perspective," *Social Research* 42 (Autumn 1975): 538–50.

Warner, W. Lloyd. *A Black Civilization*. New York: Harper & Bros., 1937.

Wasson, Avtar S. "Susceptibility to Boredom and Deviant Behavior at School," *Psychological Reports* 48 (June 1981): 901–2.

Watzlawick, Paul. *How Real Is Real?* New York: Random House, Vintage Books, 1976.

Waugh, Jack. "Main Street Nostalgia," *Christian Science Monitor*, March 25, 1972.

Wax, Murray. "Cosmetics and Grooming," *American Journal of Sociology* 62 (1957): 588–93.

Westen, Tracy A. "Barriers to Creativity," *Journal of Communication* 28 (Spring 1978): 36–42.

Whyte, William H. Reported in "Small Is Livable: Using Urban Space," *The Futurist*, June 1980, pp. 71–74.

———. *The Organization Man*. New York: Simon and Schuster, 1956.

Willis, David K. "Soviet Scourge: Hard Drinking," *Christian Science Monitor*, January 10, 1978.

Wilson, Bryan R. *Sects and Society*. Berkeley: University of California Press, 1961.

Wohl, Paul. "Soviet Youth Drinking Traced to Boredom," *Christian Science Monitor*, May 24, 1976.

Wrighter, Carl P. *I Can Sell You Anything*. New York: Ballantine Books, 1972.

Wynn, Marie. *The Plug-in Drug*, New York: Viking, 1977.

Zijderveld, Anton C. *On Clichés*, London: Routledge and Kegan Paul, 1979.

Zuckerman, Marvin. "The Search for High Sensation," *Psychology Today*, February 1978, pp. 39–43.

Bibliography

INDEX

About the Author

ORRIN E. KLAPP is Professor of Sociology at the University of Western Ontario, London, as well as Professor Emeritus of San Diego State University. His articles have appeared in the *American Sociological Review, American Journal of Sociology,* the *Journal of Communication, Behavioral Science,* and the *Journal of American Folklore.*